A VIEW FROM THE
SIDELINES

To Mona,
and to Norman and Maggi Hackett,
for all their help and advice.

A VIEW FROM THE SIDELINES

SIDELINES

MICHAEL SHEA

SUTTON PUBLISHING

First published in the United Kingdom in 2003 by
Sutton Publishing Limited · Phoenix Mill
Thrupp · Stroud · Gloucestershire · GL5 2BU

British Library Cataloguing in Publication Data
A catalogue record for this book is available from the British Library.

ISBN 0-7509-3245-7

Typeset in 11/14.5pt Sabon.
Typesetting and origination by
Sutton Publishing Limited.
Printed and bound in England by
J.H. Haynes & Co. Ltd, Sparkford.

Contents

Introduction

Nations would be terrified if they knew by what small men they were governed.

Talleyrand

Leaders of all classes and persuasions soon come to recognise that in public life perception is reality. Reputation has to be managed, for what is seen is believed to be true. If the news is bad, it grabs the world's attention more than any amount of good news, for we live in a media-dominated environment, where a quiet day is a bad one in the newsrooms, and pressurised editors decide that something has to be done about it. News does not just happen, it is made, and, to quote Dan Rather, 'if it bleeds, it leads'.

As in a public swimming pool, most of the noise comes from the shallow end, and tabloid circulation wars, plus the needs of newspaper self-publicity, demand that crises have to be created on a daily basis even where none exist. The headline-grabbing ventilation of outrage, and the governing conflicts of the moment, overrule everything else. There is always some rent-a-mouth, perpetually outraged MP, superannuated peer, or attention-seeking lobbyist to be found, ready to be inflamed by some red rag and then made to dance to the tabloids' tune. They become the hyenas of public opinion, vociferously gnawing away at the body of any fallen hero or new initiative, indulging in abuse inflation, or condemning the most minor infringement of public morality. Given the tabloid-like symbiosis between the prurient and the puritanical, even in some of the broadsheets, and the fact that people who are currently in the limelight are always more interesting than their policies – the singer counts more than the song – reputations are constantly made or broken in the pages of the newspapers, on the *Today* programme or various television screenings, rather than in the democratic debating chambers of the land. As self-denial and reticence are not among the noted characteristics of the political élite, the latter are, by their very nature, all too available to be set up, then judged, by their performances. The hidden razor wire that separates the reporter and the reported on is always there to ensnare the publicity-seeking victims if they come too close, or stay around too long. It has always been so.

In this floodlit, goldfish-bowl world, there are many serious figures, but there are lots of absurdities too, many of them politicians and other 'celebrities', created by puff artists as our role models, and further inflated by an insatiable media who follow their activities. Goldfish are, after all, reputed to change size according to the size of the bowl. So it is with leaders and others in the public eye, many of whom have been created by a process of 'image management', rather than having been born to govern. Goldfish bowl, or is it a piranha pool? The media, acting by risk-averse shoal instinct, quickly spot the savoury bait, which is the self-satisfied presumption of those who put themselves forward as tribunes of the people. The hunters naturally follow such succulent prey, according to that day's lead agenda, giving particular attention to who is at the top of the current totem-pole. The camera lenses focus on prime ministers, princes, pop stars, football heroes, their wives, or, preferably, their mistresses, then blaze a trail to their front doors, in order to flash the story, or the sound-bite (which has, incidentally, an average length of a mere nine seconds), around the world, then move on as new victims come into view. For, in that glass arena, as in international affairs, where stories of war or famine are arbitrarily picked up and then dropped, it is the iconoclastic editors, like the priests of long ago, who splash around at apparent whim, creating that day's gods and devils, defining who is in and who is out. With great creativity, they seduce with praise, then crush with criticism. They choose and enthrone our day's heroes for us, garland them with adulation, have us briefly worship them, then ritually slaughter them before our eyes. Text and image define our judgement on the lives of others.

No matter how knowledgeable and worldly we think we are, at the sound of politicians hawking their policies from the tailgates of their bandwagons, we, the people, reach across the toast for our morning newspapers, in order to reinforce our usual reactions to things, then largely accept much of what we have read. We end up with a vision of what we think the 'they' we read about are like, while, deep down, suspecting we may often be wrong. Nonetheless, we naturally tend to act on the 'seeing is believing', the 'no smoke without fire, so it must be true', scenario. In such ways are commonly shared views perceived as absolute truths.

Nothing succeeds like reputation, but reputations can be changed in an instant. When I was woken by CNN early that last Sunday morning in August 1997, to be told of the Princess of Wales' death, those with the first editions of the tabloids to hand, copies printed early the night before, would have seen that each one of them echoed those strident sirens of journalism, the females that the Princess herself used to stigmatise as 'the Wednesday Witches', or the 'Feminazis', and were among the nastiest ever. They were unanimous in screaming their red-topped condemnation of her for bringing disgrace on the Royal Family, for her behaviour with Dodi Al Fayed, and so on.

Death sanctifies. By the time the last editions hit the streets, the same newspapers had already begun to create her divine status as 'the People's Princess'.

In the chapters that follow, I take a careful but not too serious look at the reputations of a range of different people in positions of authority, how they got there and how long they managed to stay there, before being gunned down. In Shakespearean terms, some of them were born great, some achieved greatness, and some had greatness thrust upon them. As an extension to that last category, there are also the many who have been created with the help of special interest groups, aided by the puppet-masters and spindoctors of life, each with their own personal agendas. World leaders range in character from dictators with absolute power at one extreme, to those many job-holding consensus-seekers who exist as long as those around them find it convenient to keep them in place. But no matter how powerful or weak they are, they all need help in achieving their goals.

So how can we as outsiders determine the crucial difference between the real status of such individuals and their posturing, when so much of public life is like one long, carefully staged press conference? How, in particular, can we gauge the worth of politicians as they campaign for our attention, waving their most politically attractive flags, and steering their policies by the sound of our applause? Dick Crossman, lamenting that an open mind in politics was always considered irresponsible, hit the nail with precision when he commented, 'Politicians are ambitious not to make important decisions, but to say important things.'

Against that background, this book's additional aim is to look hard at some popular icons of the day, and at how the chasm is created, and defended, between the outward perceptions we have of things and the lesser reality behind the scenes. For public figures, from whatever walk of life they come, are, first of all, carefully window-dressed, by themselves or by their attentive minders, for the watchers in the outside world. Beyond the labyrinthine corridors of power, we observers may be quite certain about what we think of some famous figure, but are so only because of how they have been presented to us via the mind-colonising opinions of the media.

Most leaders do not lead. They do not even manage. They are holders of titles, figureheads at the front of the pack. Many of them could be termed marionettes, façade leaders, with little substance behind the mask of authority, yet they are frequently vested in the public mind with superhuman qualities, and become the stuff of legends. They are often very average men and women who have somehow emerged at the top, victims rather than arbiters of their destiny, carried along by events rather than determining them. But the really fascinating aspect of the process is to study the leadership team behind them, for it is this that guides and presents the outcomes. Rule one in public life, consequently, is that the real quality of any leader, in whatever sector, is usually in inverse proportion to the number of aides and image-makers on his or her staff.

In the persuasion business, even strong leaders need advice on their packaging, presentation, and strategy: tall corn must also learn how to bend with the wind. Weak leaders and organisations need to be particularly carefully arrayed in the garb of authority and wisdom by their image-makers, to hype up the public impression of action, and to hide inaction. Thus selection panels, choosing future leaders for all sectors of society, frequently opt for the ones who are or can be made most attractive to the media, rather than going for the most able. That hidden wiring in the choice process is a common phenomenon in all Western democracies.

The following telling quotation, from an anonymous pamphlet called *Mirrors of Washington*, was published in 1921.

> *An American President is selected by the newspapers, which know little about him, by the politicians, who do not want a master but a slave, by the delegates to national conventions, tired, with hotel bills mounting, ready to name anybody in order to go home. The Presidency, the one great prize in American life, is attained by no known rules, and under conditions which have nothing in them to make a man work hard or think hard, especially if the chosen one is endowed with a handsome face and figure, and an ingratiating personality.*

How about that for the up-to-the-moment truth?

Leaders rise and fall not so much over their actions or inadequacies, but over the confidence of their style, their body language, and their verbal communication abilities when they speak to their electorate. Demosthenes said that with public speaking, 'delivery, delivery, delivery' was everything. What was true for the Greeks is true today. For any public servant, speechwriting for ministers comes with the job, yet for all the elegant phrases they can dream up, it is the delivery of leadership that counts. Words are slippery things, and their meanings can get waylaid, or rubbed away by misuse or a lack of passion and commitment.

Over a forty-year career in the public and private sectors, I have seen, close-up, a huge range of prominent people of all sorts and conditions, as they polished their images in the green rooms, before going in front of the cameras and arc lights. To a greater or lesser degree, everyone in the public eye spends time arranging their carefully concerned expressions in the mirror, as precisely as they choose their ties or jewellery, before strutting the stage for public viewing. Oscar Wilde said in jest that 'a well tied tie is the first serious step in life', but he was not far short of the truth. People still expect those in authority to dress for the occasion, and though an American president nowadays can emerge from a working session at Camp David in an open-necked shirt, there was a huge outcry in the mid-seventies, when the US President, Jimmy Carter, who had already allowed himself to be seen on TV collapsing while out jogging – an image that seriously undermined his position as a strong leader – chose to give one of his famous Sunday evening television chats wearing a knitted shirt and a woolly cardigan. One top, middle-aged, New York City politician said indignantly in my hearing, 'I want my President to dress like a President when he speaks to me.'

For a surprising number of even the most powerful of leaders I have met or worked with, each morning's headlines, which offered them the world's current perception of themselves, became their daily milk of reality. That was what their careers and, what mattered more, their re-electability depended upon. By contrast, while negative profiles in the newspapers were of huge concern to them, if they did not get *enough* attention, they immediately began suffering from what I call limelight deprivation. For the blunt truth about public life is that when a name disappears from the front pages and the television screens for any length of time, its holder no longer exists, even, in a way, to the individual himself. One distinguished former government minister whom I met recently humbly wheeling his shopping trolley in Tesco's, paused ruefully in his search for chocolate biscuits, and said, 'Someone has just asked me if I used to be someone famous, and I began to ask the same question of myself!' Given the brief duration of any public shelf life, the 'where are they now?' question comes very soon to us all and our all too accepting minds. We also need to keep a firm eye on the calendar, and remember that de Gaulle said, 'The art of good government is not to allow men to grow old in their jobs.'

Inevitably, in any life, many of the most revealing and most destructive stories about people and their habits are better left untold. Discretion and loyalty insist on that, just as privilege imparts trust and discipline, and too much revelation defeats its own end. Above all, in this hindsight-assisted excursion, every attempt has been made not to be too judgemental, though I was sometimes tempted to be so by those who have hurt others.

As much political posturing is like poorly rehearsed theatre, I go on to discuss the modern preoccupation with spin, the polishing of performance and the slanting of news to better effect. Putting carefully aside until the relevant chapter my contention that today's spinners are more usually found sitting in newspaper editors' chairs than in Whitehall or Downing Street, where, on a daily basis, they weave the tales we all delight in, it is a fact that, for every man or woman who stands up to speak on a public platform, or to be interviewed by a television news reporter, there are key individuals whose only function in life is to build and massage their employer's image. The practice of spindoctoring, which often has more in common with the word spinnaker in its use of wind, has had a bad press; yet it is a totally necessary part of good governance.

Before the expression came into common use, the Americans used to refer to such advisers on public image-making as 'savvy handlers', the public relations controllers who monitored from the sidelines, or toiled away behind the scenes, to make sure that whatever position was to be presented came across to best effect. A prime minister or president might appear to make major decisions, but the work had already been carefully crafted by others, since, when the moment came to go public, it had to be seen to be right. In international affairs, when a president flies across the world to meet his opposite number, teams of diplomats ensure that the treaty is ready for signing, and that the cameras have pole position to witness the deed. Decision-formulating and decision-taking are very different functions.

None of this savvy-handling is particularly new in politics. In 1960, Theodore H. White, a close confidant of the Kennedys, wrote in his famous book, *The Making of the President*, about building up the image and myth of power and position. In Britain, such a media management industry did not really come into being until the late fifties, when the Tories took the much-mocked decision to employ an advertising company to market themselves. Labour cried shame, but soon followed suit.

Since we gauge public figures by the way in which they communicate with us and with others, the better they are at it, the more dangerous they become. Bertrand Russell wrote that 'to acquire immunity to eloquence is of the utmost importance to the citizens of a democracy'. If he were living today, he might have replaced the word 'eloquence' with 'spin'. Most serious mis-understandings, in our professional as in our private lives, are due to failures of communication, to a message badly delivered or wrongly understood. Rudeness in communication is intolerable, and the only time the most important of those written about in this book was seen to be really angry was when someone close to her was unnecessarily rude to a junior member of staff. That never happened again.

My objective in writing this book is not to write an autobiography, but to give the flavour of certain past events, the casual footnotes to prominent people in their particular settings, though for reasons of continuity the anecdotes have been firmly skewered to my own experience of the individuals involved. I have concentrated largely on past times in Berlin, and my time serving as a diplomat in Ghana, Bonn, Bucharest and New York, in that order, from which last post I was seconded from the Foreign Service to Buckingham Palace. But tales have beginnings before they begin, and ends after their endings, so I offer no apologies for including many other snapshots as well.

For most of us, past stages in our lives are a blurred recall of half-remembered events. Without a diary, and few of us keep other than engagement diaries these days, much is forgotten, of faces, of places, of incidents. We programme ourselves to disinter only the happy and the tragic highlights, the dramatic peaks and troughs. Even when we are trying to be totally honest, we embellish or fillet history to suit our present peace of mind. One well-known published diarist, now dead, who had obviously taken Mae West's advice 'Keep a diary and one day it will keep you,' keeps mentioning me, and conversations he had with or about me, and my work at the Palace. It is all very interesting stuff, but for one small thing: I never, I swear, met the man. If, in the words of the old joke, a journalist's sense of history is who bought him his last drink, in my case, more simply, history is what I remember.

I was delayed for many hours recently at Gatwick Airport, and had plenty of time to browse through many of the so-called biographies of The Queen that appeared in mid-2002, to celebrate the Golden Jubilee. Was I flattered to find myself mentioned in most of them – my professionalism or lack of it, my style, my habits, my successes and catastrophes? Possibly yes, probably not. But I was impressed by how plagiarism is obviously no crime in such writings. Author Jones lifted, almost verbatim, from Janice, Tom, Dick or Harry. Inaccurate stories became true by dint of frequent repetition. At a guess, about 50 per cent of the ones about me were true. For example, I am reported as having thrown down a challenge to James, or Harry, or Arthur that they could try, if they dared, to take photographs of the Princess of Wales when she went on holiday to the West Indies, but that they would not succeed, because of the excellent security. For the record, they did succeed, crawling through the undergrowth to take, secretly, the notorious pictures of her, heavily pregnant, in her bikini. The truth is that if such a challenge was made, it was not by me. It was, perhaps, my Canadian deputy, for I was on holiday in Norway at the time. Yet there it is, in a dozen texts, so it must be true. I have since done a trawl of another forty to fifty 'royal' books, and there are all the fictional 'truths', again, and again and again.

As neither biography nor autobiography, this book is a catalogue of observations, made from occasional past jottings, which were kept as prompts for future recollection – although I am aware that memories often offer rather messy evidence of the past. The book is also a pot-pourri of anecdotes, those short and reasonably true reflections of human behaviour, the biographical devices Churchill termed the 'gleaming toys of history'. Sometimes as observer, sometimes as participant, I have woven together a string of reflections and anecdotes, to give a different view of events and happenings, and of some celebrated individuals who have strutted their stuff on the public stage over the last forty years. They are remembered for their great public acts, refracted through the prisms of popular acclaim; but urbanity can disguise so much, and hide so much vacuity, so it is often the little episodes, the revealed asides, the half-naked ambitions beyond their reach, that give a taste of what they were really like, and what it was like to be with them. Even a glimpse can reveal the sand beneath the feet, and it is these tiny incidents and frailties that define their wit, their character, or their weaknesses. While behind-the-scenes dramas and tantrums break out over merely the colour of a tie or whether to wear pre-camera make-up (one puce nose betrayed a hard-drinking minister as an aspiring alcoholic, but its owner, a man of inexplicable self-satisfaction, refused all camouflage, to his detriment), taken together with the pomp and trappings of office, they can determine many front-of-stage events.

One or two modern writers claim to have invented the word 'anecdotage' to describe the verbal meanderings of the carpet slipper brigade. But Benjamin Disraeli used the term back in 1870, when he wrote, 'When a man fell into his anecdotage, it was a sign for him to retire from the world.' The stories that follow speak for themselves, and readers can be as judgemental as they like, though the laws of libel and slander have curtailed the telling of many true stories about the sycophants and the muck-raking journalists, who, with their own brown envelopes, no different from the buyers of peerages or other awards, ranked with the liars and deceivers who have always been there, pretending to be numbered among the great and the good. They are left in peace, for, if revenge on them had been plotted, as the old saying goes, two graves would have to be dug.

Does anyone have a reputation that outlives them? In the end all fame is transitory. To gain a reputation is the beginning of the fall, as the moments of greatest glory often contain the seeds of eventual destruction. So often the great and the good, the powerful and the feared end up, to paraphrase the wonderfully quotable Enoch Powell, 'lonely, bitter, and alone at home', or, more usually, in some forgotten corner of the local geriatric nursing home, the yawn personified, like old salts regaling anyone who will listen to past glories. When the 'great' slip from the front pages, they are soon forgotten. One former politician is remembered only when he briefly emerges, with creaking charm, to reminisce over some anniversary or other. Sometime soon we will read his obituary, and vaguely recall him in his prime. Where are any of them after their famous fifteen minutes? We do not know; we seldom care.

Proust wrote about 'involuntary memory', and as we journey into our own pasts, vast tracts of it are best left unvisited. To those of you who were present at the events I relate, do not say that you remember things differently. We all remember things differently. As Voltaire said, 'history is fables that have been agreed upon'. They travel with lightning speed around the world, changing to suit the circumstances. We all come across great stories that have been adapted to fit the person, the time or the place, so a curse on those who said clever things before we ourselves got round to it.

Let me give one splendid example of the variance of the truth. In a book written about the social pitfalls of diplomacy some ten years ago, I told my version of the story: the scene took place in the British Ambassador's residence – was it Cairo or was it Tehran? It is a grand, black-tie dinner, and the first course is cleared away. A servant drops a dish, so the floor is slippery with olive oil, and when the waiters come in carrying the main course – best Scottish beef for the thirty guests – they slip, and the precious meat cascades all over the floor. It is all rapidly removed.

A mere twenty minutes later, the butler and waiters come in carrying a new main dish, baked salmon in a wonderful dill sauce. Bewildered and impressed, the Ambassadress, who has been sick with worry since some of her guests were among the highest in the land, summons the butler and chef once everyone has departed. 'How on earth did you do it?' she asks, in praise and in awe. 'I had no idea we even had salmon in the deep freeze.'

'You didn't, Ma'am,' comes the satisfied reply. 'But that's what the Swedish Ambassador next door was serving. His guests much enjoyed the Aberdeen Angus.'

On publication of the book, there was outrage from a number of serving and retired fellow diplomats. Did I, as author, not realise that dinner took place in Prague, when Sir Gilbert Pratworthy was Ambassador, or in Tokyo, with Sir Miles Upperwurst, or with Ambassador Protochump in Paraguay. . . . Ah, well. I was actually there in Ghana, when hot, sweet, chocolate sauce, meant for the pudding, was carefully poured by the stewards over each piece of meat. . . . We all had tomato sandwiches in the end.

Here are my memories. They are meant to entertain. As no less a person than the editor of the *Dictionary of National Biography* said recently, no really good story about someone important is ever quite true. For what is truth except what you remember to be the truth?

ONE

Meetings with Dictators

One death is a tragedy, one million deaths just a statistic.
Josef Stalin

Much of life is spent waiting for others. On this occasion it is an evening in late September 1975, and we are waiting for a dictator. Outside it is cold and dark. From distant windows only an occasional light dimly shines. Power supplies are intermittent: the restriction of one electric bulb per apartment is severely enforced. Inside this building it is very different. We stand, kicking our heels, waiting at the bottom of a long, white, marble staircase. Down the middle gushes a garish red carpet. Gilded clocks are everywhere, each showing a slightly different time. Above hang sparkling, over-opulent chandeliers. This is neither Buckingham Palace nor Windsor Castle. This is the palace of President Nicolae Ceauşescu of Romania, in central Bucharest.

Dictatorship is an awesome thing. Its trappings can be evil. In that sad city it was forcefully demonstrated, on a daily basis, that pomp and circumstance and sycophantic adulation were not just the hallmarks of age-old monarchies. The cult of personality ruled. Undue deference to status is endemic in all societies, but in a dictatorship such as this it was absolute, for leaders such as Ceauşescu need to defend themselves, not just with secret police and machine-guns, not with mere spindoctors, but with mind-blowing propaganda and the richest trappings of power.

At the bottom of the stairs, and for the moment the centre of attention, stands a tense little man smoking a large Havana cigar. He is wearing a Gannex overcoat. He keeps looking irritably at his watch. Behind him hover a plain-clothes policeman and a couple of private secretaries. A huge, heavy man, Robert Maxwell, publisher to the President of Romania, who has, he tells everyone, helped fix this particular visit, lurks – unusually for him – well in the background.

We wait and wait. Suddenly, above us, we hear a commotion. Down the stairs, at a brisk pace, come a number of purposefully athletic men, dressed in cheap dark suits. At the top, a woman in a long white gown has appeared. She has greying hair, combed severely to the back of her head, accentuating an inquisitive, mean face. Elena, President Ceauşescu's Lady Macbeth of a wife, descends the staircase. In this part of the Balkans, Central Committee politicians and apparatchiks came in two versions: puce-faced or bleached grey. The insignificant-looking man, who paces behind his wife, is the latter breed, with dark eyes darting from below a thatch of matted hair. The men in the cheap suits, the secret police or Securitate, fan out around them. As they approach, the tense little man slips off his Gannex and hands it to his policeman. Harold Wilson, Prime Minister of Great Britain, stretches out his hand to greet the dictator Ceauşescu.

Both men smile, but there is little warmth in their eyes. They begin talking via an interpreter. After a few moments I take a hesitant step forward and whisper to the Prime Minister, 'The British press are waiting outside, Sir.' As the Head of Chancery in the British Embassy in Bucharest, I am the man responsible for the administrative details of Mr Wilson's visit, and I know that the press can make or break it.

'Right,' he grunts, and, without offering any explanation, thrusts his smouldering Havana towards me. 'Don't let it go out,' he says in his reedy voice, as he reaches into his pocket and produces a cold, egalitarian pipe and sticks it in his mouth. I hold the still-burning cigar carefully out of sight in the side pocket of my jacket, as Harold Wilson, the man of the people, adjusts his tie and prepares to meet the cameras.

One of the reasons for keeping his cigar burning was that no one had any lighters with them, and Romanian matches were notorious. The joke had it that if you bought a box of Romanian matches, took one and struck a light, you might as well throw the rest of the box away because you must have had the only match in the box that actually worked.

A further insight into Harold Wilson came just before the State Banquet in his honour. The Prime Minister gave instructions that he wanted someone to come in just after the main course had been served and whisper urgently in his ear. We stood bemused, waiting for further instructions.

'Just do as I say. Come in and say, "Prime Minister, you are wanted urgently on the phone, or something".'

What could we do but obey? Mere first secretaries at the Embassy were too junior to be guests, but that night I was on duty outside, waiting and watching the Securitate men at their ease. Even then it was not an easy matter to gain access to the dining-room halfway through a state dinner but an order was an order. An empty whisper was urgently delivered to Mr Wilson's ear, with Ceauşescu and various Romanian ministers, and not least the British Ambassador, staring hostilely at my daring intrusion on that great occasion. Diplomatic task completed, the Prime Minister followed me out of the door. It was his excuse to have a comfort break in the men's room, but, as every move he made was being monitored by the Romanians, his secret would scarcely have remained such for long.

As General Charles de Gaulle once said, 'Leaders have always stage-managed their effect', and he was a man who was particularly alert to the perception people had of him. Even when he left office, he was accused of 'retiring into the limelight' to his home at Colombey les Deux Eglises. Leaders showcase themselves in the search for an image, an artifice, which suits their aspirations. Communist dictators build imperial marble palaces, while middle-class democrats, wooing the working man, publicly spurn the rich man's cigar in favour of a proletarian cloth cap and pipe. Mr Wilson called public relations 'organised lying', and, given his obsession with the press, he knew exactly what he was talking about. Clever, adroit, a subtle negotiator, he always had a keen eye on the next day's headlines. We now know, from Cabinet papers released under the thirty-year rule, that he virtually invented the political sound bite, as the result of employing Cecily Berry, later to become voice coach to the Royal Shakespeare Company, who insisted on his cutting down on his highly rhetorical way of speaking and keeping his utterances short, sharp and simple. In her action plan, she told Wilson to give his words more edge, adding that he should relax his shoulders, since that showed greater self-confidence. But those who live by image, die by it in the end. If Mr Wilson coined the phrase, 'A week is a long time in politics', a better rephrasing is 'The weak are a long time in politics'. Along with a few dictators, we came across a number of them, too.

Back at the Palace in Bucharest the following day, still acting as the duty diplomat, photographs were taken as I handed Mr Wilson the leather-bound treaty documents he had come to Bucharest to sign. I stood between him and President Ceauşescu, well back from the table – I have the original photograph to prove it. But, in the next day's Romanian newspapers, mere underlings were wiped from the published press photographs as being unworthy of the greatness of the occasion. Only the two leaders are shown, seated at the table, with pens perched ready in their hands. Such is a diplomat's life: now you see him, now you don't. Ah well, Stalin had Trotsky airbrushed out of many of the great revolutionary photographs, so I was just another minor victim of a long communist tradition. Incidentally, at the end of the visit, the Prime Minister left behind a signed photograph of himself. Over the years, I have accumulated quite a collection of signed photographs, and on each the signatures still stand out. Not so on Mr Wilson's – his signature has faded totally away.

Much later I recalled that palatial Bucharest setting as we watched the grainy television film of the Romanian coup in December 1989, when communism was overthrown. Every step of the struggle for power in the new electronic age was shown live on television. We saw the man whose staff had airbrushed an unnecessary figure out of a photograph, standing on a balcony alongside his crone of a wife, being heckled by the crowd for the first time in his life. Then, as if part of a dramatic feature film, the two of them were seen escaping, by helicopter, from the very rooftops of the presidential palace.

For weeks after Ceauşescu's overthrow, Studio 4 of Romanian Television became the centre of the provisional government, where each broadcast by the dissident poet Mircea Dinescu became a public act of the new-found democracy, while the new leaders jostled over such absurd issues as who had the most prominent place in front of the camera lens.

Later, again watching television in a lonely hotel room in South Africa, I saw a couple of huddled figures as they were filmed being dragged roughly out of the back of an armoured car, still believing the myth of their ultimate popularity.

'My children,' the woman could clearly be heard appealing to the soldiers who surrounded her. 'You know me so well: I am the mother of your nation.'

I could barely recognise Ceauşescu and his wife Elena. Only in close-up, once their bloody bodies were lain out on the snow, was it possible to recognise the man who had led to my burning a hole in my pocket with a prime minister's cigar.

Was Milton correct? Do 'they also serve who only stand and wait'? In public life one has to think on this on frequent occasions. This time, some time in the mid-sixties, the standing was very much on the sidelines, waiting, not for a dictator-president or for a prime minister, but for a dictator-emperor. As the so-called desk officer for pan-African affairs in the Foreign Office at the time, I had been despatched to Addis Ababa in Ethiopia to strengthen the British

Embassy's coverage of the Organisation of African Unity Conference there. Even diplomatic observers from an unpopular country – Britain had fallen out with most of the Dark Continent over Rhodesian sanctions – were invited to the opening reception given by Emperor Haile Selassie, in a huge, ornate audience chamber, larger than in any palace in Britain or Bucharest.

The reception guests, mainly African or Ethiopian, stood in a single line, backs against the walls of the great hall, waiting for the Emperor to arrive. To gain entry in the first place we had had to walk through a huge marble doorway, at either side of which was chained a live leopard, which, in feline terms, was an indicator of what was to come. One of the beasts was quite frisky, but, reassuringly, the chains allowed us, with care, to walk unharmed between their rapacious claws.

We waited and waited. Perhaps an hour passed in a silence disturbed only by low, reverential whispers. At last the distant sound of a dog's impudent bark echoed into the audience chamber, followed fairly soon by its owner, a corgi, a personal gift to the Emperor, it was said, from the British Queen. This precocious animal prowled imperiously round the room, eyeing us all up and continuing to bark at the wide-eyed guests. Then, unbelievably, a chained lion entered, held in uncertain tether by two tall, very black Nubian servants. The word slaves should be avoided, though it would probably have been a more accurate description. The lion limped, for, according to further hearsay in a town where verifiable facts about the Emperor were in very short supply, it had been shot through the foot in the 1960 attempted coup.

Corgi, limping lion, then a very fat, almost round man, the Minister of the Court, appeared, walking daintily backwards into the middle of the reception room. Then, and only then, came the diminutive, dapper, bearded Emperor, the Lion of Judah himself, son of Ras Tafari, wearing the most immaculate pinstriped suit. Today's Rastafarians, with their dreadlocks, would have marvelled at the meticulous appearance of their revered icon, and, doubtless, vice versa. At his entrance, every Ethiopian in the room, and a fair number of the other African guests, immediately prostrated themselves on the floor. As almost the only European, I must admit to having felt more than a little ill at ease, recalling no guidance notes in the diplomatic protocol book on the etiquette of prostrating oneself in front of an Emperor. All was well. My modest bow in the direction of the Emperor did not lead to my being thrown to the lion for insufficient deference to that absolute ruler.

Elsewhere in Africa, and another desert kingdom, twenty years later. In life many human emotions are experienced, amusement, passion, astonishment, awe, but only occasionally, if one is lucky, does one see real fear, fear, in this case, in the eyes of a Moroccan head of protocol. We had had a hard day. The Queen had had to sit in a hot, open-sided tent in the middle of some huge tract of sand, watching demonstrations of horse- and camel-manship. There was little hardship in that, but then, for several long hours, we waited for lunch with King Hassan, or, more correctly, waited for him to turn up before lunch was allowed to be served. No explanations for the delay were forthcoming. It was hot, very hot, and it got more than a bit ill-tempered, not least because the large travelling press party was camped directly opposite us, a mere thirty feet away, very much unshaded, watching and photographing or filming our every move and impatient expression.

'It is difficult to exaggerate the gravity of the situation, but I shall do my best,' is an ancient journalistic joke. The journalists in this case had reason to be even more bad-tempered than we were, as the headlines and the photographs were to prove the next day, as each journalist vied with his neighbour in describing how badly they, and, incidentally, The Queen, had been treated. If, as some of us had privately wished, we had all stood up and stormed off, the journalists would have had a field day, and good luck to them. But one way or another we got our lunch eventually, though the problems of the day were far from over. There was to be a State Banquet in The Queen's honour that same evening.

At the appointed hour, The Queen emerged from the Guest Palace and climbed into the back of the waiting Rolls-Royce. Members of the Household, as usual, scrambled to get into the cars that were lined up for the suite. Police escort cars took up positions to the front and the rear of the royal convoy. Then absolutely nothing happened. No movement. We waited a couple of minutes. Private Secretaries jumped out and started asking pertinent questions. We were all rigged out in full white tie and tails, which is not the most calming dress for a balmy Moroccan night. Starched collars wilted. Tempers began to steam.

The Chief of Protocol arrived, also white-tied and tailed, his matching complexion banishing his natural skin colour. 'His Majesty King Hassan is not yet ready to receive Her Majesty. Would Her Majesty be kind enough to return to the cool of the Guest Palace and wait till His Majesty is ready?'

A request, not a question. Her Majesty is a person of great calm. Never, almost never, did one see her angry. Tonight she was not angry; in fact she looked the coolest of us all as the senior Household gathered outside the open door of the huge Rolls-Royce to gauge her reaction. No, there was even a sparkle of amused determination in her eyes. She was going to do no such thing as return to the Guest Palace. She had had enough. Queen, evening dress, sparkling diamond tiara, arms folded, very determined. Her Private Secretary, emulating her cool by turning cold, if not icy, put his point of view to the Chief of Protocol in no uncertain terms. The latter, by this time, was giving an excellent impression of a snail over which some schoolboy had tipped a packet of salt.

The King was no simple dictator. He was known for his tyranny. He had suppressed his enemies with an age-old ruthlessness over many decades. He had had to, in order to survive. Rumour had it that he had personally put some rebel leaders to death. He was an absolute monarch. Many European tourists, travelling to Morocco during his reign, will remember having been thrown out of the best hotels and the best suites without any warning when he and his court suddenly decided to visit Marrakesh or Tangier. That night, the expression about being between a rock and a hard place suddenly took on a new meaning for the Chief of Protocol. The

British Monarch was not to be bullied. The man saw no future in his future. He tried to plead, to explain, to get us to understand that his King brooked no negatives. We felt a brief twinge of understanding for him as he was dispatched to sort things out, and quickly, in two minutes flat, or the British Royal Flight would be summoned and we'd be comfortably tucked up in bed at Windsor by the early hours.

We could not but notice the unbridled fear behind the rivers of sweat that cascaded down the man's face, while the constant wringing of his hands, for once, made that metaphor most appropriate, since liquid from them dripped to the ground in front of him. But we had had a long day, and had already received frantic phone calls from London, warning us about the next day's equally steaming headlines; so all sympathy evaporated. Finally, a terse call from the Private Secretary to the Moroccan Prime Minister, another deeply unhappy man (for in despotic monarchies even prime ministers are easy to replace), resolved the problem, and a good evening was subsequently had by all.

Thinking of hands wet with salt brings to mind another pair, belonging to another dictator, whose plump hack of an employee, from the *Mirror* newspaper, rang me at home one evening. The journalist was choking with excitement. He claimed to have discovered that the Austrian-born Princess Michael of Kent's father had served in the SS during the Second World War. It was something that I needed to check very rapidly, for in this life anything is possible. A call, full of apologies for bothering her, was put through to the Princess. She was told about the newspaper's story. There was a sharp intake of breath: to cut a long story short, it turned out to be true.

Before the first editions were on the street, the *Sun* was on to the story as well, and was preparing to run it as its own 'exclusive' front-page lead – such a situation was, and doubtless still is, quite common, since both tabloids, used to chasing each other from sensation to revelation in pursuit of greater circulation figures, had paid spies in each other's newsrooms. To prevent anyone in the Palace Press Office having to spend all night on the telephone, we acted as always when the media needed to know something quickly, and put out an agreed statement to the Press Association. Every newspaper now had confirmation of the story, along with the Palace's comments. 'No further statement will be made,' we added hopefully.

Captain Bob Maxwell, the overwhelmingly brutal proprietor of the *Mirror*, whom I had first met in Bucharest a decade previously, rang me up. He, like his hack, was choking not with excitement but with an autocrat's fury, which caused his vocabulary to become very limited. A man known as much for ruthlessly stifling opposition as for eradicating it, often on apparently irrational whim, was apoplectic with rage. Men and women who had worked for him were at first mesmerised, then terrified by the sort of primeval power he exerted over others. His mood swings, from huge charm to the blast of fury, punctuated his days. In a demented tirade, coarse with swear words, I stood accused of everything under the sun, but in particular of 'betraying my paper's exclusive' to the *Sun*. 'How dare you!' bellowed this minor, but very frightening dictator.

Relieved that we were speaking on the telephone and not face to face, I politely told him that we were not interested in his exclusives, and that, in any case, traitors in his newsroom had beaten us to it. His renewed tantrum was wondrous to hear. At home, wife and small children gathered around, open-mouthed, as the bold Captain's tirade erupted from the telephone earpiece. He threatened to have me sacked, or, punishment of all punishments, marched in front of the Press Council. Reason was tried in an attempt to counter his spluttering rage. Eventually he was told that the phone was about to be put down on him. And it was.

Fast forward to the next evening, and a glittering reception at the Italian Embassy in Belgrave Square. On my arrival, Captain Bob spotted me from afar and advanced towards me – he was, after all, the man who, it was currently joked, would ring Megalomaniacs

Anonymous to announce, 'It's me!' He was notorious for getting his own way by bullying or by sacking; so what verbal, if not physical danger was I now to be subject to? Not being particularly brave, but with lots of distinguished witnesses around, I decided to stand my ground.

There was no need of bravery. 'Michael, my dear chap. How good to see you! How *are* you?' A bear-like arm embraced my shoulders and a huge hand squeezed my arm. 'Come,' he said, escorting me across the room. 'I want you to meet Neil [Kinnock] and Roy [Hattersley].'

In those days, and things have changed little, Labour needed the *Mirror*. The politicians turned to greet Maxwell, all smiles. At the top of a short flight of steps, his huge bulk towered above them. He was wearing a large ring. He extended his great hand to them, knuckles, curiously, turned upwards. Wondering if he was offering them his ring to kiss, later I said as much to a laughing Neil Kinnock. We would not have dared joke with Bob Maxwell.

I thought of his split personality, and of his huge hands, when I read the press speculation that Captain Bob had clung for a long time to the rail of his yacht before he fell into its engulfing wake.

To demonstrate that the arrogance of the dictator is not just a primitive or foreign phenomenon, I offer one more glimpse of a domestic mini-tyrant from my Palace days. This time it was somewhere in England, with a Chief Constable who hated the press. He told me that he was not going to agree to any of the arrangements I had made for the royal visit to his parish. He would not have it, he said, looking at me as if I were depriving some village of its idiot. But I would not have it, and I won: his kindly, fearful deputy, gave me a whispered warning to back down, which I ignored.

The Chief Constable took me aside after the stormy meeting, grasping my upper arm in a vice-like grip, less friendly even than Captain Maxwell's. 'Don't ever stray into my territory after you've left the Palace, Shea, or I'll see you done for,' he hissed. I have seldom seen such hatred in a man's eyes. He meant it all right.

11

Though we may think we are immune, we are often dictated to by others, or, more precisely, by the views of others from our distant past. The 'Give us a child at seven and we will have him for life' claim of the Jesuits rather resembles Keynes' contention that even practical men are slaves to the ideas of some long defunct economist. Even at a light-hearted level, few of our most strongly and stridently held views have not been purloined from elsewhere in our pasts. Decades ago, when I was a student in Edinburgh, there was a well-known guy called Harry Bell who was always being quoted as the key authority on politics, on the sexual revolution of the sixties, or on the best Rose Street pubs. He constantly cropped up in our conversations, and new entrants into our clique would rapidly be introduced to his autocratic ideas and opinions. And Harry had ideas on everything: he was the ultimate purveyor of all wisdom and of all prejudice.

'Bumped into Harry at the Abbotsford last night and he was wickedly critical of American policy on Vietnam. . . .' ' Harry's found this great new pad and is thinking of buying it. He says we must all buy property, following Mark Twain's dictum: "Buy land, they've stopped making it".' 'Harry Bell's advised me to change tutor . . .', '. . . to shave off my beard', '. . . to dump my girlfriend'. Harry was the ultimate dictator. Outsiders, when asked if they knew him, would nod their heads vigorously. Of course they knew Harry.

The trouble was that Harry Bell did not exist. He was a figment of our undergraduate imagination, our way of sending up strangers, our own sub-Masonic secret. Despite that, Harry took on a life of his own, and later he found a wife and children, and obtained two rather good degrees, ending up in some mysterious relationship with British Intelligence. He had come from a croft near Inverness, which he had inherited from his parents who were long dead, but now he had a rather exciting flat in Chelsea. How the hell could he afford that? He would even write postcards to some of us, with his typical and at the time trendy 'Hi guys!' from far-flung parts, mysteriously matching his handwriting, his dogmatic opinions, and his travel plans with those of one or other of our little group.

Fiction, like life, is full of invented maiden aunts, and external dictatorships imposed upon us. 'I'd love to be with you on the fifth, but sadly, my tyrant of a boss has arranged a meeting, and insists that I'm there.' Like a sudden death, or the funeral of a close relative, such things allow us to avoid work or extend play. Harry was better than all these, a friend in need, a consolation, a dictatorial adviser, as we stood, poised on the threshold of post-university life. Maybe I should find him again, and have him insist on taking precedence in my plans. He could come in quite handy this Christmas. I wonder if he's still got that flat in Chelsea?

Lord Reith, the founder of the BBC, when reputedly asked what his preferred form of government was, replied to the effect that it was despotism, tempered by assassination. President Nicolae Ceauşescu and Emperor Haile Selassie suffered the second part of that definition. But words can assassinate too. Few have confronted fallen dictators as skilfully as the leader of the tiny handful of crofters that were left after the Scottish Clearances, in the latter days of the nineteenth century: when that autocrat and arch-clearer the Duke of Sutherland asked him to help raise a regiment to fight in the Boer War, he replied, 'You have preferred sheep to men, Your Grace. Let sheep defend you.' The words echo down the years with stunning simplicity.

TWO

A Scramble for Africa

If you want to test a man's integrity, give him absolute power.
Abraham Lincoln

As Lincoln's words remind us, integrity and power do not always make good bedfellows. Poor post-colonial Africa has proved to be a great breeding ground for tyrants as well as for malaria-carrying mosquitoes, which in my days in Ghana were almost eradicated. The continent's perverse leaders have not all been of the ilk of Bokassa, or Idi Amin, or Mugabe, but each, in their turn, has parodied a long-vanished imperial past, often leaving the pageantry of their former colonial rulers far behind. Uniforms, decorations, and the gleaming orders of rank garland them as they once garlanded our viceroys and Governor Generals, as well as Mussolini and Goering. But it is not just such trappings of perception that keep the people in their place: it is, as with Zimbabwe's 'War Veterans', also fear, bred from mob rule.

When I returned to my room at the university at Legon near Accra that hot and humid November day in 1963, I found that someone had fixed to the door of my room, with four brutal, rusty nails, a large hand-painted slogan which read, 'Death to Imperialism and Neo-colonialism. We the working people create all material values.' I still have the poster. Several words are misspelled, but the effect remains dramatic, since the red lettering runs down the sheet like blood.

I remember the day so well, for it was shortly after I had arrived in Ghana, flying in late one night from London, having hardly ever flown before, to be greeted by a blast of oven-hot air as the doors of the aircraft opened and I descended into the blackness of an African night. But I was immediately captivated, particularly when, sitting over some welcoming cold rum drink on the tropical balcony of the friendly diplomat who met me, I heard for the first time the Ashanti drums beating incessantly in the far distance.

My memory tells me that my borrowed car had already broken down, and so that morning I went by bus from the university's campus to the High Commission in Accra, to make arrangements for a familiarisation trip I was planning to the north of the country. When I climbed into the rickety bus it was fairly empty, but when it stopped at a suburban village, a comfortably gigantic African lady took the seat beside me. No problem in that, except that she then proceeded to roll down her whole top and suckle two fairly large children she had with her. Even by pressing myself against the half-open window of the bus, I could not escape her expansive abundance, as my shirt was later to reveal. She was cheerful enough though, and we chatted amiably all the way into the town.

Late that afternoon, I returned to the university to which I had been dispatched by the British Foreign and Commonwealth Office, to learn about the newly emerging, 'revolting' as the elderly joke had it, Africa, and, in particular, to attend the Institute of African Studies there, to do some research for my PhD on emerging African economies. This time, travelling in some state in a High Commission official car, I found on arrival that I could not drive right up the long slope to the main university buildings. President Nkrumah, or, more importantly, his party commissars, were currently inveighing against the ivory tower élitism of the university, its students and its academics, and, in my absence, the 'masses' had stormed the university to make their popular discontent effectively known to the much-criticised black intelligentsia. Not too much damage was caused to the buildings, and whether my room had been singled out for that blunt, ill-spelled anti-capitalist message, I never discovered.

I was far from the only European studying at the university at the time, so perhaps it was mere coincidence.

Various other cherished moments are stored from that special day. As I walked back down the hill to the Institute of African Studies late that afternoon, Thomas Hodgkin, its Director and the husband of Nobel Prize winner Dorothy Hodgkin, was sitting in a wickerwork rocking chair on a first floor terrace, surveying the demonstration as if watching the Gold Cup at Ascot. He was sipping something cold from a long glass. Beside him, also in a rocking chair, was the nuclear physicist, Professor Alan Nunn May, who was by that time Professor of Physics at the university, a post given to him by Nkrumah following his release from years in prison – he was one of the notorious spies who had betrayed the West's nuclear secrets to the Russians. In true communard style, that committedly Marxist professor was also being served with a long cold drink by a white-coated, white-gloved Ghanaian steward, all very proper and pastiche colonial. As they sat there on the terrace, rocking away in tandem, setting a scene of ironic brilliance in the rays of the setting sun, I heard one murmur to the other, 'Beautiful demonstration . . . so well organised . . . just what these people need.'

The steward at the Institute was forbidden from calling the white staff 'B'wana'. I had tried to stop a friend's steward calling me B'wana, which was a ridiculous colonial inheritance, particularly since his brother turned out to be the Dahomeyan Ambassador to Ghana, and he often had to ask for the evening off to attend diplomatic functions as a guest. He also rather liked cockroaches to eat, but that is another matter. His response to my egalitarian request was always to agree. 'Yes, Sir, B'wana. I no call you B'wana in future. No B'wana. What you like to drink, B'wana?' I gave up.

That other voice of reason in those turbulent African days, when the Russians and the West were busy fighting for the minds of its leaders and its youth – both inevitably failed – was Dr Conor Cruise O'Brien, who had previously served as the UN's representative in the Congo to controversial effect. As Vice-Chancellor of the University of

Ghana, his leadership qualities were to be well tested. To this day, his seriously brave address to a meeting of students is well remembered: following the 'masses' brief occupation of the university, he exhorted all academics to defend liberty and freedom of expression to the bitter end. It was one of the most notable and least spun speeches I have ever heard; and, for once, under pressure, his every word came simply and unadorned.

As a shrewd observer of some of the absurdities of international diplomatic-speak, in his book *To Katanga and Back*, O'Brien wrote about the terms used by delegates to the United Nations, in their efforts to bring peace and eventual independence from Britain to the troubled island of Cyprus. One brief report concerned the British representative trying to argue that when Her Majesty's government offered 'self-determination' for Cyprus, it did not mean 'independence', but 'self-determination'.

The UN's wonderfully experienced simultaneous interpreter was defeated, translating the carefully differentiated English words into French on the lines of, 'When HMG offers independence for Cyprus, it does not mean independence, but independence.'

The early sixties generated great excitement in Britain about all things African. Many books and publications were devoted to that continent, both in defence and in criticism of the events that were so quickly engulfing that variously talented, tribally riven area of the globe. It was a period of high political correctness, and Britain's attitude to Rhodesia was beginning to dominate in terms of our refusing to countenance calls for economic sanctions against that country, and also against the developing apartheid regime in South Africa. In consequence, as a new entrant into the diplomatic service, rather than being sent off to learn some difficult language such as Chinese or Arabic, I and one or two others were sent off to learn what we could about post-colonial, sub-Saharan Africa. Much good it did us, or Africa. It was a decade before that respected British Africanist, Sir Martin Le Quesne, wrote his famous dispatch, 'Africa – does it matter?' with a sadly modified 'No' as the answer.

This was the period in which President Kwame Nkrumah, among the first and most talented of the African independence leaders, became alienated from the British government, largely through the single-minded antagonism of the then Commonwealth Secretary, Duncan Sandys. Sandys believed that anyone, in particular any African leader, who was not with us, was against us. In consequence, in simple terms, most of the newly independent African states were driven into the willing but hopelessly ineffective arms of the Russians. And it was not just Africa. The LSE-educated Jamaican Prime Minister, Michael Manley, told me that he found Sandys so patronising he used to switch off his hearing-aid every time he came anywhere near him. Nkrumah, meanwhile, surrounded himself with a selection of dubious advisers, including a handful of hard-line British communists, which further alienated him from the mother country, a term, incidentally, that was still in common use back in London.

There was a partly absurd, partly horrendous cult of personality in the Ghana of the time, with Nkrumah constantly referred to as 'Osagyefo', meaning 'the Redeemer', giving him an almost godlike status. Photographs of him were doctored to show light or even a halo around his head, and there were daily headlines with strong biblical overtones, such as 'the earth trembled as he spake', or 'He leadeth us into a new dawn'. Other less serious headlines jostled for position on the same page. I have the 'trembling earth' one alongside an article under the striking banner headline, 'We must crush nudity', attacking those Ghanaian women who were still so primitive and shameless, according to the newspaper, that they went topless when they did their weekly washing in the rivers or lakes. And who could blame them for their practicality, including, as my inexperienced eyes saw on more than one occasion, the better endowed of such women tossing their elongated breasts over their shoulders out of the way as, bent double, they got on with their tasks.

As a result of a century of missionary zeal, biblical phraseology was much employed elsewhere in Africa too, as it still was a decade later, in Malawi, when President Hastings Banda, an Edinburgh-educated doctor, was asked by an impertinent Western journalist if it were true that he had threatened to skin his enemies alive.

The President's reply was sharply dismissive. 'How could I be accused of such a thing, I, an Elder of the Kirk of Scotland!'

Headlines of another sort heralded a new impetus behind Marcus Garvey's 'Come Back to Africa' movement in the early sixties. As a result of his call, a handful of black Americans had arrived to study at the university in Ghana while I was there, as descendants of slaves and would-be returnees. It was a far from successful pilgrimage, and few of them found anything in common with their African cousins when they got there. Take Harvey for example. He was a six-foot-six, ex-professional basketball player from Harlem. Huge in every way, he was always angry and aggressive, but we got on well enough for some reason, perhaps because he sympathised with me as an expatriate Scot, since I too had been an obvious victim of English imperialism. He dated exclusively with the few white women around, and showed little interest in any of the black students.

One day he dragged me off to a tirade of a rally held in Accra by the revolutionary American, Malcolm X, another demagogue of the age. His philosophy was that 'it's the hinge that squeaks that gets the grease', which was a true enough argument. I was the only white face in the crowd, and I have a newspaper photograph to prove it. Few of his listeners understood much of the philosophy behind the speaker's words, but that did not matter: it was the high-decibel revolutionary tone that provoked the cheers. 'Yes', Malcolm X thundered. 'The Black Revolution is coming. It will be controlled only by God. Revolutions won't be won by singing "We shall overcome". Revolutions can only be based upon bloodshed.' Harvey also dragged me to a Ray Charles concert, where I heard the blind singer's 'Take these chains from my heart and set me free . . .' and I have been a fan of his ever since. How could I not, with all the tear-stained faces, including mine, around me?

Harvey cried like a child once more when I broke the news to him one dinner-time that President Kennedy had been assassinated. He went quietly home thereafter.

Meeting Nkrumah, which was to happen soon after my arrival, I found him charm personified – the kindest face, a wonderful smile that was white with teeth, in comparison with the grey and yellow British ones I had grown up with in the forties and fifties, and lively, sparkling eyes. He had that rare thing, charisma, and he was one of the few African leaders who had been invited to stay at Balmoral by The Queen. One could not go anywhere, in any government office in Ghana, without seeing a photograph of The Queen standing with him outside that baronial Scottish castle. Presented to him at a reception, I was introduced as that suspicious oddity, the British diplomat who had come to Ghana to study.

'So,' said the President, 'I hear you are a member of the British Foreign Office, Mr Shea?' It was still in the days before the Office was merged with the Commonwealth Relations Office.

'Yes, Sir,' I replied.

'So you've come to spy on us?' he said with a further beaming smile.

'To learn, Sir,' I said, or something equally trite.

'You know what we always say: if we send our children to London, particularly to the LSE, they come back communists. But if we send them to Moscow to study, they come back as capitalists. What will you go back to London as, Mr Shea?' he asked. I fumbled for words and he did not wait for my reply.

These were turbulent times. There were demonstrations almost every day outside the British High Commission in Accra, with all the usual anti-neocolonialist slogans being paraded on banners, including one uniquely strange one, straight from one of the current copies of *Private Eye*, reading 'Sunken Glands go home'. It must have been a totally incomprehensible slogan surely, except to a small handful of Brits who would be aware that Duncan Sandys was so named because of a never proven relationship with the infamous Duchess of Argyll. At her divorce trial, a notorious photograph of a naked man was passed around the courtroom. The man was headless and his physical attributes were peculiarly misshapen. Poor Duncan Sandys: it was a strange slogan to see paraded through the turbulent streets of Accra.

Accra also gave me my first brief exposure to the cynical world of television journalism. I was a witness when a group of African protesters politely asked an American television crew to stop filming them till they could go off and find a British flag to burn in front of the cameras. Of course the television crew obliged. It reminds me of an occasion, much later in life, when a camera crew, filming a press conference I was giving in Kuwait, asked me to move away from a house, because, uniquely surely throughout the wider world, some pro-American graffiti was painted on the wall behind me.

Despite the jokes that had long circulated about the British Council sending morris dancers to Africa as part of our cultural export drive, we were never anything like as inept as the Russians could be. I was among the audience on the famous occasion when they flew out the Bolshoi Ballet to Accra, or at least part of it, along with a fairly large orchestra. They performed in an open-air stadium, late one afternoon when it was still very hot and sticky and the crickets were at their noisiest. I was seated with the Western Diplomatic Corps, several rows back, while the front rows were largely occupied by Party loyalists, though not the President himself, surrounding a self-satisfied looking Russian Ambassador and his Embassy colleagues. The rest of the audience were Ghanaian, the men in their stunning kente-cloth togas, the women in their rainbow dresses and turbans. We were all genuinely looking forward to an uplifting cultural experience.

It was, I think, a series of excerpts from *Swan Lake* and a number of other ballets. The orchestra started up well enough, though the strings had constant tuning troubles in the heavy humidity. And then, oh joy, the ballet dancers appeared on stage, the males in their white tights and bulging codpieces, the women in their tutus, posturing elegantly, gracefully, through their wondrous routines. Not a single Ghanaian there would, I suspect, have seen classical ballet before. Their national dancing was of another pace, the popular 'Highlife' hypnotic, super-charged and rhythm-filled, 'the vertical expression of horizontal desire' that had been theirs for a hundred years. Mouths agape, they were not prepared for this spectacle of Russian culture at its best.

Gradually, however, the white tights on the men started to turn see-through with sweat in all the wrong places, and the tutus began to wilt. The dancers bravely continued against all the odds, but first one Ghanaian lady then another stood up and started clapping, and from then on it built up rapidly, until the whole crowd was swept into a billowing storm of laughter and cheering at this most absurd of sights among the dripping palm trees. Even those sternest balletomanes among us Europeans began to see the funny side. In a very short space of time, the whole audience had erupted into a wildly delighted throng, men and women standing and dancing in the aisles, aping the more obscene absurdities of dress that they saw on the stage, overwhelmed with joy by this spectacle of inappropriate Western culture. At about this time the Russian Ambassador stormed out, followed meekly by his fellow diplomats, and the performance rapidly came to a sticky close. So much for Russian hegemony.

The cult of personality in Ghana, created by the local spindoctors of the time, created a semi-godlike figure out of a pleasant, charismatic, but sadly misled man. Nkrumah, Osagyefo, was soon to be overthrown in a coup. But, in the meantime, Ghana broke off diplomatic relations with Britain over Rhodesia. The High Commissioner and his staff were expelled, a decision that was postponed and postponed because there were so many good Christmas parties coming up. Eventually, we were seen off at the airport by half the Cabinet, all of them bearing flowers and presents, and many of them in tears. Such is Africa.

Other glimpses, other places. In comfortable middle age one remembers, almost with awe, the derring-do of youth, when without a care, we travelled widely in Francophone, and, as the joke had it, Anglo-saxophone Africa, from Accra to Timbuktu, then on to

Niamey, and via part of what is now the trans-Saharan rally route, to the remotest of the remote desert towns of Agadès. Agadès is the centre of nowhere, but it has given its name to a very special crucifix, the Croix d'Agadès, the top part of which is a loop rather than an upright, mixing several religions in that one device. Three and a half decades later, Michael Palin arrived there, and, from his brief description, little seems to have changed, with the Grande Mosquée, a strange pyramid of mud and sticks, still the only building that is more than two storeys high. The flat-roofed houses – we slept under the stars on the roof of the little French-owned hostel not only for the cool but to escape the teeming hordes of cockroaches – were almost indistinguishable from the burning sands that surrounded them. The inhabitants were almost invisible too, though it did not stop us being fined by a solitary policeman for going the wrong way down a totally deserted street. From thence we went north, in temperatures of over 100°F, to Tamanrasset in Algeria, before driving back across a southern Sahara littered with the bleached bones of cars and long-abandoned army trucks, via Niger, one of the poorest countries in the world, then finally to Fort Lamé, the romantically named but easily forgotten barrenness of a town, in Chad. I still have the brutal and not always too helpful document I carried, as guidance for British Embassy and High Commission staff serving in Africa at the time, which warned us that while driving through these countries, if we hit anything, animal, adult or child, we were strongly advised not to stop, but to drive on to the next police station and then report it, otherwise we might be 'chopped' there and then. We were even more careful with our water supply, and very precise in taking our bearings while driving across the Saharan piste, going from huge white-painted oil drum to oil drum, the French Army's route-markers in the desert. If we missed the next one, which was usually five kilometres distant, we rapidly retraced our route before the wind obliterated the tyre marks in the sand, and took a new bearing. I was once both moved and frightened when, coming across a high dune, I suddenly saw, etched against the sky, a huge cross of remembrance, fashioned out of a steel girder as the upright and the chrome bumper of the car as the crossbar, to mark where the vehicle's young British occupants had recently died of thirst.

I had been travelling with other adults in those days, people who knew the terrain, and I was young then. I was much more alert to the dangers of the African wilderness years later, for by then I had acquired a wife and two small children, who were playing happily in the back of a cheap Japanese four-wheel drive when we broke down at dusk in northern Kenya, in the semi-desert, far from our intended destination. Tribesmen with spears and an array of wild animals came out of the gathering gloom to stare at us, and I realised then my limitations, not merely of my mechanical skills. But suddenly a single, solitary army vehicle, the first we had seen in hours, came up and its kindly sergeant driver mended the defect, and set us on our way once again.

On my own I visited Liberia, land of freed slaves, which, in those days, was also known colloquially as the Firestone State, since the Firestone Rubber Company owned and controlled most of what went on in that so-called liberated land. William Shadrach Tubman was president at the time, and the whole place was so corrupt that the American Ambassador revealed that even he had had to tip the doorman at the presidential palace in order to get out after an official call. Biafra, in Nigeria, was also on my list, where, later, a Scottish university friend who was teaching there, had to smuggle his cook out hidden in the boot of his car to avoid his being slain in the subsequent bloodshed.

Much further up the coast, Sierra Leone was in those days a pleasant enough place to be. The economy was booming, the people were well fed, the roads in reasonable repair, and elementary education was available to all. The telephones sometimes worked, and no one was in danger of being mutilated in tribal massacres. The Durham University-educated Sir Milton Margai was the nation's president. He had a wife who, if memory serves correctly, was a blonde barmaid from Wigan who never set foot in Sierra Leone. When Milton Margai died suddenly, chaos and revolution had to be prevented until his brother, Albert, presently on an overseas trip, could be brought home to take over the reins. What to do? The story persists that when rumours of Sir Milton's death began to circulate, his civil servants stuck his dead body upright in the back of the presidential Rolls-Royce, packed it round with bags of ice, while a faithful aide hid below the level of the windows and swung the corpse's arm back and forward as if Sir Milton were still alive and waving to the crowd. They drove him round and round Freetown until brother Albert arrived to ensure the family succession.

Then there was another visit to Emperor Haile Selassie's Ethiopia, where I had again been sent to cover an Organisation of African Unity Conference. We had, at that time, a most conspicuous ambassador there, Sir John Russell, the son of the famous Russell Pasha of Egypt. Sir John was known throughout the Foreign Service for his splendidly eccentric dispatches. In one, he accurately described the Ethiopia of the day as a country that had 250,000 priests but only thirty-one doctors, the priests teaching a doctrine that the earth was flat, with the Ethiopian Church known to celebrate 'Saint Pontius Pilate's Day'.

My image of myself as a gallant diplomat of the old school, briefly suffering for his country's cause in such a hardship post, was put to rest on the day after the conference had ended by Sir John sending me off one morning, in a Land Rover, with his driver, away from Addis Ababa at a mere 8,500 feet, to the even higher cliff tops overlooking the source of the Blue Nile. Everyone else in the Embassy was busy, so I had to go on my own, and because it was quite a distance, a packed lunch was provided for me.

Verdi got it all wrong when he had Aida sing about Ethiopia, 'the verdant country of my birth', as a place of deep forests and cool lakes and rivers. Reaching my very barren destination, we parked the Land Rover under the shade of a lone and desolate tree, and I stood and marvelled at the scene. The vegetation-free, inhospitable crags below me were spectacular, swarming as they were with apes, while, on closer examination, the rock face was pitted with a thousand caves, many of them inhabited by the hermit priests of the Ethiopian Church. I gazed spellbound, oblivious to the prospect of a simple picnic of sandwiches and mineral water, unaware that meanwhile the Embassy chauffeur, who had been wearing a khaki jacket for driving, had produced from the back of the vehicle a smart folding table and chair, a white tablecloth, silver, glasses, a hamper and a coolbox filled with fine white wine. But he was not yet ready for me. He carefully took off his khaki jacket and put on a white steward's tunic, rich with crested brass buttons, folded a white napkin over his arm and bid me to my seat under the shelter of that great lone tree on the escarpment, with the Nile, a mere trickle, a thousand dizzy feet below me. I had forgotten my camera, so only the curious apes, and one solitary, silent hermit in brown sacking rags, peering at me over a rock, were witness to the scene.

A day or so later, Sir John took me out riding early one morning, across the foothills behind the Embassy. I remember our coming to a crest and seeing what looked like a large telephone pole, with a sturdy crossbar, outlined against the morning sky. From it were suspended two long black bundles, coated in what looked like tar. I turned enquiringly.

'Yes,' said Sir John, 'two corpses, *pour encourager les autres*,' or rather to discourage them, for those who trespassed against the Emperor and were found guilty were hanged out there, blowing in the wind, to remind other would-be wrongdoers of the penalties of treason. Much good it did the Emperor when, eventually, they crept up on him by night to smother him and most of his family with pillows.

I visited an Ethiopian prison during that particular trip, accompanied by a Scottish professor who was lecturing in law at the university, and was shown the barren shed where they executed the guilty. My guide took me into a corner, and, carefully pulling aside a canvas sheet, revealed a dusty electric chair, with, on the side, a neat plaque reading 'A Gift from the United States government'.

The story was this: the Americans, in an early burst of doing the decent thing in the horn of Africa, had decided that the traditional

Ethiopian method of execution, whereby the guilty person was either dragged off his feet by a platoon of soldiers using a length of rope that was wound round the neck and then thrown over a beam, or else pulled apart by four wild horses galloping in opposite directions, was not a tidy way of doing things. So, after both the British and American Ambassadors had had to protest to the authorities when, in a fit of modernisation, they employed Land Rovers or Jeeps to replace the horses (for some reason it was deemed to be a negative marketing statement by the car companies concerned), they suggested that an electric chair might be a tidier way of disposing of the guilty.

The only problem was that when the first unfortunate victim was strapped tightly into the chair and the switch was pulled, all the lights of Addis Ababa went out. Disappointed, the prison guards quickly ensured that the man was neatly thrown from the nearest high roof.

Sir John Russell was also brave. I was there on the tense occasion when the Embassy's compound was invaded by fierce local demonstrators, who, once more, were protesting against Britain's Rhodesian policy. The Embassy guards, who were Sudanese, were withdrawn by us, since their presence would merely have added to the tension, so we diplomats lined up beside the ambassador on the Chancery steps, in symbolic hope of keeping the mob at bay. Eventually the ambassador climbed up on top of the bonnet of his Rolls-Royce, a piece of carpet carefully positioned between his shoes and the paintwork to stop any scratching, and bellowed at the crowd, 'You can demonstrate where you like, but please get off Her Majesty's rose bushes.'

African vignettes – happy and tragic, hopeful and hopeless, threatening and infinitely kind. Sir John told some jokes, made the ringleaders laugh, and then served them glasses of tea and little cakes. Good humour prevailed and the crowd evaporated.

THREE

Hello to Berlin

In War, the truth must be accompanied by a bodyguard of lies.
                                                    Winston Churchill

If Africa has been one lifeline, Berlin has been another. Now there are huge trees, half-century-old trees in the Tiergarten. Back in the mid-fifties, it was a desolate wilderness, for everything that would burn had been cut down and taken away as the citizens had tried to keep warm, to cook, to survive. I have just come back from that city, from strolling along 'Unter den Linden', from ambling curiously through the Brandenburger Tor, from visiting the strangely dated museum at Check Point Charlie, from standing where the Wall had stood, from watching through a crack as a man casually splashed red paint on to a harmless piece of concrete, to sell later to tourists as a piece of the graffiti-daubed real thing, from visiting the new British-designed Reichstag, from viewing the still dilapidated streets in the former East Berlin, where the old Chancelleries of the Third Reich once dominated half the world.

My love affair with Berlin goes back to the mid-fifties when I was posted there as an eighteen-year-old national service second lieutenant in the Intelligence Corps. Called up straight from school, I had no experience under my belt apart from two brief summers working as an assistant male nurse at what was then called a 'mental hospital' near Glasgow, a beautiful Victorian pile from outside, and a bleak and sorry prison within. It is a story of another age, and two of us were sent to Coventry when we complained about the treatment that some of the so-called nursing staff doled out to the inmates, most of the former acting like the petty criminals and misfits that they were, while the latter were either heroic relics of the traumas of the Second World War or were suffering from acute syphilis, which led to what I think used to be called a 'general paralysis of the insane'. I was also disciplined for daring to do anything other than shout orders at the patients, for I had tried to talk sensibly to one old sea captain and hear his reminiscences, when I had thought no one was watching, even though he kept repeating that he had 'got that way' by having personally gone up to the crow's nest on his ship to look for any sign of submarines, and, 'when I climbed down again, my ship had gone'.

In the army, we emerged first from months of basic training at cold Catterick Camp in Yorkshire, a bleak time of boots, bull, blanco, and bromide in the milky tea, to keep our natural instincts at bay. I have disliked milk in tea ever since, though I especially hated the coffee, which was made in the huge tea urns on Sundays. From there the conveyor belt led on to Officer and 'Let's try to make gentlemen out of you' Cadet School, eventually to my arrival in Berlin, which welcomed me warmly, offering a wildly decadent utopia of excitement and high living.

I had known about 'the Germans' long before I knew what Germans were. My earliest memories are of huddling under a stairwell in central Glasgow during the Clydebank Blitz – it was the most fortified place to be – sitting on my mother's knee, making up a little song with her in time to the exploding bombs. This was apparently to console me for not being allowed to play with the buckets of sand that were positioned there, as elementary anti-incendiary measures. I vividly remember one night, seeing my father – a ship designer, and thus in a reserved occupation, who consequently served as a senior air-raid warden, and always wore a white steel helmet – come off duty with blood streaming down his face. No, not German bomb damage but a hysterical Glasgow woman whose child had just been killed by shrapnel, attacking the first person she saw in uniform with her nails. And was the last remaining bottle of pre-war whisky consumed that night?

For the island city of Berlin, the mid-fifties was one of the coldest periods of the whole Cold War, so, professionally, it was an exciting time for a young British officer. The shadows of a past war, highlighted by untouched acres of ruins, starkly identified the continuing threat of future conflict, and, even in my humble role, I came across strange doings of espionage, of secret communications monitoring operations known as Sigint, and of mysterious and legendary bodies known as Brixmis and Soxmis. These were the British and Soviet Military Missions, the former based in Potsdam, which, though closely monitored, were allowed to travel freely around each other's territories, as so-called confidence-building measures. In truth they were no more than official spies, for the extreme secretiveness of the East German regime, which was under the total control of the Soviet KGB at the time, made most other intelligence gathering very difficult indeed. There were whispers, however, of that most secret of secrets, the tunnel, code-named Stopwatch/Gold, which the Americans had cleverly dug, a whole half mile in length, right under the border with the Soviet Sector, to the point where they had placed advanced listening devices directly beneath Russia's main communications centre, and the cables that ran from it under the Schonefelder Chaussee. Allen Dulles, the then head of the CIA, described the project as one of the most valuable and daring projects his organisation had ever undertaken. It was finally completed in 1955, shortly before I arrived in Berlin, and for some time a huge amount of information was retrieved from the microphones installed there, in particular the names of a significant number of Soviet spies who were then operating in the West. Inevitably, as was later revealed, the Russians got to know about the tunnel fairly early on, probably via the notorious British spy, George Blake, a consular official who had been brainwashed after his capture in Korea. From then on, they cleverly used the system to provide damaging disinformation to the Western Allies. In the secret world of espionage, when real secrets are unearthed, whether about Soviet Berlin or Al Quaida, the greatest care is taken to ensure no one discovers what is known, or when it was known, or all the high-tech skills and human spies are immediately compromised.

I had driven up to Berlin from my Army headquarters near Cologne, in an ancient Opel Kapitan that I had just bought from a fellow officer. With time for only a few driving lessons, the Major who tested me told me, in no uncertain terms, that I could not drive, but added helpfully that I doubtless would be able to do so by the time I reached Berlin. He then handed me my driving licence. It was an exciting journey, particularly getting through the *Autobahn* checkpoints across East Germany. Even in my youthful naïvety, I realised that as a British Intelligence Corps officer, in uniform, driving through their territory, I was being followed the whole way. I could of course have travelled overnight on the military train; but what fun would that have been, given the firm rule, imposed by the East Germans, that the blinds had to be pulled firmly down all the way to prevent unknown secrets being seen?

Berlin was sex and sin, the overhang of the past, and the reality of the present. Sally Bowles and the sinister master of ceremonies in the film *Cabaret* were yet to be created, but Christopher Isherwood's *Goodbye to Berlin* and *Mr Norris Changes Trains* were on my bedside table. Days were taken up doing strangely tedious work with index cards, checking the backgrounds of possible communist sympathisers, but the remembered nights were of visits to steaming nightclubs, which were mostly off-limits to other ranks. The girls all seemed to wear fishnet tights up to their armpits, and the sex was plentiful and cheap. Only once did we get into trouble, in our own minds at least in those less liberal days, when we realised that in one club the beautiful girls and strippers were all transvestites. Like the guy in the film, I discovered that only when one of the 'girls' lined up to relieve herself at the next 'pigs ear' in the Gents.

When we walked along the city's pavements in our uniforms, some of the older Germans still stood aside, or went into the gutters to give us right of way, even though that particular military government rule, strictly imposed after the fall of Berlin to ensure the subjugation of the defeated, had long been done away with. More vividly, I remember chatting to the middle-aged German woman who cleaned our officers' mess. She had been a school-teacher before the war, and had suffered dreadful hardships afterwards, not least multiple rape by Russian soldiers. But nothing had been so dreadful for her as having been forcibly bussed to Belsen, with a number of other professional Germans, by the British Occupation Army, some few days after the liberation of that vile camp. They had been marched past the huts and made to see the pits still full of bodies, yet to be buried. She cried as she explained, in faultless English, that she was still sometimes physically sick when she thought about it. A few days later she disappeared from the mess; she had been arrested as a suspected Soviet spy.

One memory rises above all others. It is of a group of us going into the Soviet Sector to attend the Staatsoper one evening. It was a cheap place to discover culture, and, on my basic £25 a month pay, which also had to cover my mess bills, it was a major blessing. We drove off into the East, wearing, as usual, our officers' uniforms that were supposed to allow us to go anywhere we liked in all four Sectors of Berlin. I have no record of what opera it was, but I clearly recall coming back to the mess afterwards, having driven past the Brandenburger Tor, and reporting to the duty Captain that 'They seem to be building some sort of wall beside the Gate.'

The Wall itself was only constructed in 1961, but during my time there, barbed wire fences ran along the line that separated the Soviet from the three Western Sectors of Berlin, and as early as 1957 they did indeed build a breeze-block barrier adjacent to that famous gate, the beginnings of what was to become the symbol of a Germany divided.

It was fun being a national serviceman in Berlin in the fifties. East Berlin called us back more than once, and I heard the famous Lotte Lenya sing songs from the *Dreigroschenoper* in some black-walled cellar one evening, along with a medley of other songs composed by her first husband, Kurt Weill. She was no beauty, but she had an amazing voice and magnetism: the place was packed; and was the ghost of Brecht, who had only died the previous year, sitting in the sidelines watching her too? Afterwards we came home loaded with cheap records of their songs, bought at black-market rates. I have them still.

Not even bushes grew in the Tiergarten then. Everything had been cut down for firewood, ten, fifteen years earlier, and the *Wiedergutmachung* – the reconstruction programme – was still in its infancy. During my most recent visit, close by the Brandenburger Tor, the only thing I recognised from my Army days was the Russian War Memorial, the statue of the heroic soldier, surrounded by green painted tanks, inside one of which is cemented the dead body of a Russian soldier. The memorial looks shabbier now. In those days it was immaculate, the one place in the Western Zones where the Russians insisted on coming and mounting an honour guard every day. Those were the days when the high walls of Spandau still contained a military gaol and the one remaining prisoner of the Third Reich, Rudolf Hess. At Russian insistence, all four Allied powers took it in turn to guard the prison and its lonely inmate.

One of our professional tasks was to examine specimens of printed propaganda that the East Germans and the Soviets were using in an attempt to unsettle the inhabitants of the Western Sectors, and to persuade those in the East not to flee. They were often crude, distributed in the streets, or sent to people's houses, but sometimes they could be as compelling as a modern spindoctor's line. Their function, too, was all about perception, and, to the people of a metropolis who had suffered so grievously, they appeared to offer the hope of a fairer and more secure future in East Germany.

It was in Berlin that I first saw a man hit in anger, by authority. As members of the Intelligence Corps, we drove around in little Volkswagens, commandeered from the defeated German Army at the end of the war. But unlike our colleagues from other British military units who had theirs painted army-green, ours were a sinister black. One day I was detailed off to visit the French security agency, the *Deuxième Bureau*, in their offices some distance away from Berlin's ruined Olympic Stadium complex, in which my officers' mess was one of the few habitable buildings. I drove there with a senior colleague, parking outside a steel door which was set into the side of an anonymous concrete building. I rang a bell. A narrow, barred inspection hatch opened in the door, and a pair of eyes scrutinised us. I identified us as I had been told to do, with the words, '*Intelligence Britannique*'. To a nineteen-year-old, those two words sounded spy-story wonderful.

The big door opened. We were taken in and shown around, including the prison cell complex, where, in a bare room, they were interrogating some poor French army cook who had deserted and then absconded to the Eastern Zone. This was doubtless because he had been revealed as being homosexual, which was the usual reason for defections in those less tolerant days. As we watched, a French officer hit him almost casually across the side of the face with his riding crop. I winced. I did not understand the questioning; it was too fast and furious. The man was crying, and his hands were handcuffed behind the wooden chair on which he was sitting; below him the floor was wet. Again the officer hit him on the side of the head, a little harder this time, but it had its effect. The prisoner started gabbling out his confession.

Afterwards, over a civilised glass of wine at the French officers' mess, I hesitantly questioned the need for violence. I was harangued. What would I do if I were in Cyprus right now (it was 1957), with others of my National Service intake, and supposing that we had captured an EOKA terrorist whom we suspected of having planted a bomb? If time was of the essence, would I not hit him if it would mean his confessing where he had planted it? Would I also not use force to save British lives? Who was I to condemn? *They* knew: they had life or death problems in Algeria. Where did justifiable violence begin and end? That moral dilemma has remained with me ever since.

Remembering the ruins of the Olympic Stadium that surrounded our mess building, where we could still find huge chunks of the concrete and steel swastikas that had once crowned the main stand lying forgotten in the rubble, I have found photographs of a group of us high-spirited young officers playing a childish game of hide-and-seek amid the tunnels and walkways of that once great amphitheatre. Where history should remember the glories of international sport, we are only ever shown film of huge Nazi rallies that were held there.

Berlin, then, ten years later, Bonn: there is a current joke about a British and a Russian General meeting sometime shortly after the end of the Cold War. The Briton says to the Russian, 'Over the last fifty years I have been taught that you were the enemy, and for the last fifty years you have been taught that we, the Brits, were the enemy. We were both wrong. It's the French.' There has always been much truth in this, at least in diplomatic terms, both in regard to Britain in Africa, and then Britain in Europe. This was particularly so in the period from the mid-sixties on, when President de Gaulle did so much to prevent Britain's entry into the Common Market of the Six.

That single factor dominated much of the diplomacy of the time, particularly to me, a First Secretary, dealing with economic affairs, unexpectedly posted to serve in the British Embassy in Bonn, that village on the Rhine grown big, which had been so well described in John le Carré's book *A Small Town in Germany*. I say unexpectedly, for *The Times* had printed a criticism of my being posted there; they thought it an odd move by the Foreign Office personnel department, as they had somehow found out that I had just gained my PhD in African development.

Had not Chancellor Adenauer been born in Bonn, the capital of the Federal Republic undoubtedly would have been located somewhere more convenient. As a young diplomat, whose only overseas experience so far, apart from that artificial period of military service in Berlin, had been in tropical Africa, I arrived at the Embassy having carefully packed away all my tropical clothes. In exchange I purchased, second-hand from Moss Bros, a so-called Stresemann outfit, named after the great German statesman. This comprised a short black jacket and striped trousers, which, I was assured by an elderly colleague, I would certainly require when, for example, I paid my first official calls at the German Foreign Ministry. But the very month I arrived the Ministry abolished the practice of such formal dressing. I have the outfit still.

The British Embassy, an unimposing and graceless office block, had been built on the understanding that it would be sold on when the German capital moved back to Berlin, something that in reality was to take another quarter of a century to achieve. Sited on the noisiest road in the city, with a field of sheep on the far side, it was dominated by its diminutive ambassador, Sir Frank Roberts, a man whose size was in direct contrast to his perspicacity and vigour. He had already had a most distinguished career, having dealt directly with Stalin and with Hitler in the past. His rise to fame had begun with his appointment as Private Secretary to Ernest Bevin, and was confirmed by postings as Ambassador to Yugoslavia, NATO and the Soviet Union. Most of his colleagues were afraid of him, except for two in the Embassy, one the Political Counsellor, Lance Pope, a German expert who had spent most of the Second World War in a Nazi concentration camp. He was a close friend of Chancellor Willi Brandt, so much so that when Brandt was enthroned as Social Democrat Chancellor of the Federal Republic in 1969, Pope and his wife sat on the balcony beside Mrs Brandt, watching the ceremony. In my lowly army days in Berlin, the city had a military government, but among the up-and-coming young Berlin politicians was the much talked-about Brandt, who had served with the Norwegian forces during the war, and, unbelievably, had first entered the city, whose most famous governing mayor he was to become, wearing Norwegian army uniform.

The other fearless figure in the Embassy was a British First Secretary of German Jewish extraction, Wilhelm Cohn. He, with his colleague in the American Embassy, who came from a similar background, was largely responsible for the legal aspects of the divided Germany, and in particular of Allied military rule in Berlin.

These two diplomats would sit with the German Federal team, all speaking in heavily accented English, though German was their common language: as Dr Cohn said, it was 'a matter of protocol, to keep reminding them who had won the war'.

Sir Frank Roberts' wife was an invincible lady of part Lebanese descent. She, too, played a hard game, particularly when it came to the French government's obdurate stance against Britain's entry to the Common Market. One sparkling night as she left the French Ambassador's residence in Bonn, she kissed her hostess goodnight, then, with calculated verbal dexterity, added the words, 'Thank you for a wonderful evening, my dear, but such a pity about your soufflé.' The two ladies reputedly never spoke again.

The Second World War should have been largely forgotten by the mid-sixties; nonetheless, one diplomatic colleague got into a great deal of trouble by getting engaged, and then married, to a German girl whose father had been in the SS. His choice of spouse led to his early posting away from Germany – the British Foreign Office could still be very unforgiving. In my own bachelor days, I rented a magnificent apartment to the south of Bonn, at Rolandseck, overlooking the Rhine and the Siebengebirge, a view that had been painted for centuries. But when domesticity overtook me we moved to a house owned by Herr von Brentano, a former German foreign minister. There, late one night, up in an attic where we were storing some packing cases, we came across shadows of the past when we found a hidden bundle of papers, several of which had swastikas and Adolf Hitler's signature all over them.

Diplomats, civil servants, aides and other advisers spend much of their time waiting for their principals, not while they prepare for significant events or to say great things, but while they put on their make-up, straighten their carefully chosen ties, or practise their suitably grave or confident expressions in the men's room mirror. They know that they have to look the part, for, as Laurence Olivier once said, if you can fake sincerity, you can fake anything: in public life, as in advertising, sincerity is a commodity that can be bought and sold like everything else.

It was in Bonn that I first had to wait for that major manipulator of perception, the former Prime Minister, Harold Macmillan, some years after he had left public office in 1963. Each junior diplomat in the Embassy was delegated to look after one or other of the VIPs who came to Germany when Chancellor Konrad Adenauer died in 1967. Excited to be sent to meet Macmillan, I only knew the reputation of the man whom the cartoonists had delighted in naming 'Supermac', and whose sardonic wit had been particularly praised when, in September 1960, at the UN in New York, Nikita Khrushchev, the Soviet Premier, interrupted a speech Macmillan was making by taking off his shoe and banging a table with it. The Prime Minister had coolly responded, 'I'd like that translated if I may', which brought the house down. Working in a sometimes rather staid bureaucracy like the Foreign Office, I had been much taken by his other well-known remark, 'By all means rebel, but only on one issue at a time.'

Bonn airport was tiny in those days. I was nervous, for we British have a habit of treating the great and the good not just with respect but with undue deference. Despite the rain, the great man was coatless, and came slowly down the steps from the aircraft in fully tailcoated funeral garb, as I stood there nervously, umbrella opened, waiting to greet him.

He shook my hand, smiled, thanked me for its protection from the rain, and said, 'I felt no Prime Minister of Great Britain, past or present, could ever again come to this part of Germany flourishing a rolled umbrella.'

Macmillan, unlike Wilson, but like that other umbrella man, Chamberlain, who waved his after the appeasement meeting with Hitler in the late thirties and declared 'peace in our time', was Hollywood's central casting dream of what a British Prime Minister should look like. He had his little vanities: he always used to tuck the top ends of the butterfly on his black bow tie under the tips of his dress collars, a tiny fashion statement of liberation.

When, in the car to the ambassador's residence, I routinely suggested that Chancellor Adenauer would be a difficult act to follow, Macmillan quoted the French statesman Talleyrand, 'The graveyards, Mr Shea, are full of indispensable men.'

Then he added, as an aside, that at a State Banquet he had attended given for Adenauer some years earlier, The Queen had asked the Chancellor how he liked the wine he had been served. He reputedly made a face. *'Ich schike Ihnen etwas'* (I'll send you some). It was the ultimate put-down.

A further poignant glimpse of the past was afforded me when I went with my next-door neighbour on a Rhine pleasure steamer one warm, sunny Saturday. It certainly was a Saturday, because my new found friend had to think hard whether he would accompany me that day, it being the Sabbath, and he an Orthodox American Jew. He was dressed, as always, in a long frock-coat and a big black brimmed hat, with hair ringlets dangling below. He came, nonetheless, breaking the Sabbath, and we happily boarded the noisy pleasure boat, where lederhosen-clad bandsmen, umpa umpa-ed out their tunes, while rustic Germans danced happily around the deck with flagons of beer in their hands.

How could I not have realised what an impression my friend's appearance on board would make? He was a sudden black spectre at the feast, and the spirit of the party-goers was rapidly dashed, so much so that they threatened the stability of the boat as they huddled as far away from him as possible. My American colleague understood better than I did the effect he was having, and so we decided to disembark at the first port of call, just south of the ruined remains of the famous bridge at Remagen, where the Allies had first pushed their way across the Rhine.

I should have known all this since I had been to school at Gordonstoun, which had been founded by the German Jewish refugee Kurt Hahn. After being imprisoned by Hitler, Hahn had to leave Germany in the early thirties, and took with him a small group of pupils, including the future Duke of Edinburgh, to found his school in the remoteness of northern Scotland. There were several German Jewish refugees still teaching at the school when I went there, and I remember, always, the common prayer at assembly,

'Never let me become one of a hard-hearted mob where pity and compassion fear to raise their heads.' The school's motto, '*Plus est en vous*', was a Belgian Resistance motto once seen by Hahn painted on a wall in Brussels, and adopted memorably for the school he founded.

Two and a half decades after demob, I returned to Bonn and then Berlin on my first overseas trip as a member of the Royal Household. So much had changed, and from the vantage point of the glamorous State Banquet at the Charlottenburg Palace, given by the governing Mayor, Dieter Stobbe, Berlin looked and was a very different city. The Queen had already been to Bonn and toured round the Federal Republic of Germany, with David Owen, the British Foreign Secretary, as the accompanying Minister. It was not in the latter's nature to enjoy following meekly round as part of the royal suite, so he decided that he would stay behind in Mainz, or return to Bonn, to have talks with his German opposite number, Hans-Dietrich Genscher, and also with Helmut Schmidt. No harm in that, but he and the German Foreign Minister were on the next plane to Berlin when they saw, on television, that a million Berliners had turned out to greet The Queen wherever she went.

Political opportunity is never to be missed, but some things come to nothing. We flew to Kiel later that afternoon, where the *Britannia* was waiting to take us through the Canal during the night, to be ready for the next day when, with appropriate symbolism, Her Majesty, the British Queen, was to review the German fleet, lined up in her honour in the North Sea. That morning dawned, but nature treads easily on such great events, and a dense fog prevented us from even seeing as far as the bow of the royal yacht itself.

FOUR

The Cold War Continued

Words, like bayonets, are natural persuaders.

Romanian saying

Life is what happens when one is making plans for something else. The Cold War was still being waged, both in perception and in reality, when, some years after leaving Bonn and with a break in the Foreign Office and at the Cabinet Office in London, of which more later, my next posting was to the Embassy in Bucharest. Though economically and politically not as impoverished as it was later to become in the dying throes of communism, it was a difficult and scabrous place in which to exist. All the decent food was imported in refrigerated trucks – almost all decent food, since bribery was a way of life, and, for hard currency, excellent cream and bottled water could be obtained locally. In that manipulative society, if you knew someone with sufficient access to the cellars of the Central Committee of the Communist Party, or the Romanian Orthodox Patriarchate, good wine could also be purchased for dollars or, for some reason, cartons of 200 Kent cigarettes. Oh, and caviar! That too could sometimes be bought on the black market. One teatime, at the house of our one and only family of Romanian friends, caviar was served, which our young daughters, aged around three and six, dismissively referred to as 'fish jam'. They did not much

43

like it, a fact recalled by a famous exhortation from my wife, 'Eat your caviar up, or there'll be no stories at bedtime!'

No spindoctors were needed in Ceauşescu's Romania, for the cult of personality was enforced by squalid and draconian laws that ensured that nothing like a free press was allowed to exist. The newspapers printed what they were told to print, which was mostly the complete text of four-hour-long speeches by the President, plus articles on tractor production, enlivened by pictures of happy workers standing around looking happy. Some lived in a different layer of life, and the families of members of the Central Committee of the Communist Party luxuriated in a high-walled compound with its own school, club and shops, where everything was available. To keep them happy, foreign diplomats were offered their own country club, with swimming pool and Romania's only (nine-hole) golf course. For the rest, it was what was available in the markets, or the black market. The no-joke joke was that if you saw a queue, you joined it, then asked what you were queuing for. It might just be a welcome consignment of sugar from Cuba.

There was another class, the expatriate businessmen, who bribed their way through customs by placing a new copy of *Playboy* on top of the clothes inside their suitcase – that, or those ubiquitous 200 Kent cigarettes. If the superior official did not want his cut, the customs officer merely removed the items and looked no further. It usually worked.

Of the very bottom of the rung in this communist paradise, I can offer two glimpses: one of gangs of ancient women, dressed in rags, as if in some primitive charnel house, pushing huge metal barrows through the night, clearing snow from the streets; and in my second view of hell, in a high wind, a long section of hoarding in the centre of a wide main street in Bucharest blew down, to reveal, far far below, gangs of convicts staring up at us from where they worked, lived and slept, digging by hand some waterlogged subway for the greatness of the new Romania.

It was not my first experience of corruption and convicts. From the well of memory I again see chain-gangs of black prisoners working on the roads of a southern state of America in the 1960s, and recall driving with a friend and his daughter through South Dakota about the same time. A traffic cop pulled us over for speeding. My friend, before he climbed out of the car to confront the officer, took a twenty-dollar bill and carefully folded it into his driving licence. When he got back a few minutes later, penalty free, and we drove off, my friend turned to me. 'Know what the cop said?' He smiled thinly.

I waited.

'Hope your little girl didn't see you do that. Don't want to corrupt her, do we?'

Watching film of Ceauşescu's overthrow and assassination recalls the days when the President of Romania was all-powerful. But it was his unflaggingly devious and difficult wife, Elena, whose insistence, in the mid-seventies, on increasing Romania's population – making both abortion and birth control illegal and punishable by imprisonment – that led to an appalling number of babies being abandoned to the infamous orphanages, which so shocked the West after Ceauşescu's death.

The communist system seemed invincible then. Romania was a place where a third of the population were spies or members of the secret police, the Securitate. Bugging Western diplomats' flats was commonplace. In our apartment alone, British experts, flown out to check on such things, found thirteen bugs before deciding there was little point in digging out the walls any further. We were advised that if we wished to conduct any secret or private conversations, we should do so either inside the secure room at the Embassy, or walking in one of Bucharest's pleasant parks, where, with care, one could avoid being overheard.

We were tailed everywhere. On long car journeys our young children would play a grown-up version of 'I-Spy' by challenging each other as to who would first spot the Romanian-assembled Dacia car that the Securitate agents always used to follow us. One night, arriving back at the diplomatic block where we lived – it had a permanent military guard outside, supposedly to protect us, but actually to stop Romanians getting unauthorised access – our younger daughter bounded from our car along the pavement to give a close-up wave to the two agents who had followed us all day, and whose car had now parked some twenty yards behind us. Running back to retrieve my daughter, I saw, to my amusement, that these much feared secret agents were sheltering from the attentions of this tiny child by reading a copy of the Party newspaper, *Scintea*, upside down. Such were the dictates of anonymity.

Telephones were routinely tapped, and, on one often talked-about occasion, my wife, having just telephoned an American friend, picked up the phone to make a further call only to hear the whole of her previous conversation played back to her. Some poor technical hack had thrown the wrong switch.

One of the most taxing problems for our permanent security tail must have been the long trip my wife and I made to the far north and west of the country with a Romanian professor friend. We went first to some of the wonderful painted monasteries in Maramures, staying overnight in several, sleeping on raised stone slabs, and were summoned not by a bell but by the beating of a suspended wooden beam, or tocsin, to eat with the monks or nuns. The diet was usually a simple one of bread and fish, though as guests we were given the body of the fish. As most of Romania's catch was exported to gain foreign currency, however, the monks themselves sat down to plates that held one large lump of bread and some *mamaliga*, or maize porridge, on which had been placed a large fish head that stared with dead but sinister eyes upwards towards heaven. At one such haven, the Mother Superior, a formidable lady, welcomed us in the grandest of manners. She walked aided by a long staff with a silver top, which matched her entire set of perfect silver teeth, like a villain in a James Bond film.

We moved on from the monasteries to the Danube Delta, where we left our car and embarked on open wooden longboats, propelled first by outboard, and then, when the water-lanes became narrower, by oar or by pole, to thread our way through that vast watery estate, populated mainly by pelicans, towards the remote town of

Sulina. In those days it was only reachable by water, for it stands balanced on the very edge of the delta, where it pours into the Black Sea. Apart from the food we had brought with us, our sustenance again was fish, this time caught fresh and made into instant soup by the boatman, who cooked it up, with brown water from the river, in a tin on a fire which he lit in the bottom of the boat.

Once upon a time Sulina was destined to be a huge free port, a true Europolis, but that dream had died many years earlier. Once, too, there had been a little British community there, long since perished. There was still a tiny, abandoned British church, and, more poignantly, a British graveyard, the stones telling their own stories. One old Romanian was building a magnificent tomb nearby, with marble columns and floors. We spoke to him and asked who deserved such a palace of the afterlife. 'Me', he replied. Elsewhere the graves were British, with English inscriptions. One was dedicated to a man, 'The Butcher of this Place', while others were of female 'entertainers', come there doubtless to help service the port or its sailors; and, finally, there was one lonely inscription to a British seaman who had died at sea but had been brought, as his last request, to be buried on dry land next to the church. The only problem was the water table: dig down a foot, and the pit immediately becomes flooded, so, despite all his shipmates' best endeavours, the sailor was still buried in a watery grave.

And our escort of Securitate? We glimpsed them behind us, again as in a Bond film, zigzagging in and out among the tributaries, but otherwise leaving us in peace. We knew our professor friend would be picked up and interrogated after our return to Bucharest, but as he had spent eighteen years in prison, and eight of those in solitary confinement ('I may be seventy-five, but I take away these eighteen, so I am only fifty-seven'), he declared that it was nothing for him to be worried about.

Visiting political firemen were a constant problem to the Embassy, to be handled with great caution. Many an ambassador, having given some obscure backbench MP less attention than he or she thought they deserved, would hear their complaints later, via an indignant letter to the Foreign Secretary. Such visitors were generally found difficult to please in inverse relation to their importance back at home.

While I was in in Bucharest, a famous Scot arrived as a British Council guest. I agreed to invite him for dinner, along with a senior member of the Central Committee of the Communist Party of Romania; he collapsed, out for the count, with his head in the soup, before the staff had time to clear away his plate. Nought out of ten to the British Council for not letting me know that the man was an alcoholic.

Kipling aficionados will know that his poem 'Pagett MP' encapsulates the frustrations of those working overseas who have to put up with people of that ilk. The final stanza goes as follows:

> *And I laughed as I drove from the station, but the mirth died out on my lips*
> *As I thought of the fools like Pagett who write of their 'Eastern trips',*
> *And the sneers of the travelled idiots, who duly misgovern the land,*
> *And I prayed to the Lord to deliver another one into my hand.*

This is Kipling at his best, and it should be pinned up in every Chancery as a reminder of the whims of visiting pundits and their half-inch deep knowledge of local wrongs and injustices.

There were only two decent hotels in Bucharest, one the Athenée Palace, made famous by Olivia Manning's *Balkan Trilogy*, and the other the Intercontinental. The Intercontinental was a huge new block, with a notorious nineteenth floor, banned to all: it housed the technical experts whose duty it was to bug every other room in the building.

Delightfully embarrassing occasions would ensue when a British politician arrived at one of those hotels, and immediately fell victim to the 'honey trap' – the Securitate were expert at introducing them, in one way or other, to the beautiful women who were always readily available, waiting in the foyers. One well-known visiting British MP rushed in to see me early one morning, realising, in the sober light of day, that his love life of the night before had almost certainly been recorded, if not secretly filmed, in his bedroom at the Intercontinental. An anonymous and threatening phone call to his room had just confirmed this. We put him on the next flight home to London. He immediately confessed all to his Chief Whip, and, when the Securitate tried to blackmail him later, he was, it was reported, able to laugh in their faces, and tell them that everyone knew already, and that, in any case, if the film was made available, his friends and colleagues would undoubtedly admire his prowess. There is a coda to this episode: the Intercontinental sent on his bill via the Embassy – it was for a double room.

All the Soviet controlled states were good at setting honey traps. Many will remember when, in the eighties, some of the marines guarding the US Embassy in Moscow gave the KGB a more or less free tour of the whole building in return for sexual favours offered by their beautiful female agents. There is also the now well-known story, which was only being whispered about when I first joined the Foreign Office, of my Deputy Secretary, the dry and meticulous Sir Geoffrey Harrison, as Ambassador to Moscow, flying himself home and resigning over a brief dalliance with a Russian chambermaid at his Embassy residence.

Perhaps more apocryphal is the story of the British businessman who, arriving in Bucharest, booked himself into the Intercontinental. Alert and self-confident, he believed himself an expert on all matters to do with technical surveillance, and so spent the first hour of his stay carefully searching his bedroom for bugging devices. After inspecting the light fixtures, and looking behind each picture, he came to the carpet and lifted one corner of it, finally tracking down a suspicious looking metal plate in the middle of the room. This surely must be a bug, since it was held in place by several screws and a funny wire was sticking from it, so he carefully unscrewed the screws with his penknife, causing the chandelier in the room below him to plunge downwards and break into a thousand pieces.

One verifiable story is the case of the American Ambassador's shoe. The US Embassy's technical experts had tracked some weak radio signals which indicated a listening device, but the signals kept moving around, and after many tests the experts declared themselves baffled. Days of research passed, and teams of other experts were flown in from Washington to assist. Eventually the bug was found, carefully embedded inside the leather heel of one of the Ambassador's shoes, doubtless inserted when they had been sent for repair.

In the seventies, Romania was still, relatively speaking, the good guy of Eastern Europe. Ceauşescu was nothing if not a patriot, and the Romanian Orthodox Church flourished largely because it was so ethnically and purely Romanian. Their Patriarch and the Chief Rabbi – Romania still had a sizable Jewish community – were both members of the Central Committee of the Communist Party. Ceauşescu had at one time been brave in the eyes of the West, addressing a million Romanians in Bucharest's central square, when he roundly condemned the Soviet invasion of Czechoslovakia. He refused, even in our time there, to let members of the Soviet Embassy leave central Bucharest without permission, because Romanian diplomats serving in Moscow had similar restrictions placed upon them. By contrast, we Western diplomats could travel more or less where we wanted.

President Ceauşescu used to invite foreign ambassadors accredited to Bucharest on a bear shoot, when various traditions were followed, including the ritual beating with birch twigs or the like of anyone who had shot their first prize. On one occasion it was the Hungarian Ambassador who made the first kill, and Ceauşescu took up the bundle of twigs to administer the flogging, but then paused and threw it at the Russian Ambassador with the words, 'No, you do it, Your Excellency. You're much better at beating Hungarians.'

Not only Harold Wilson, but also Mrs Thatcher, as the then Leader of the Opposition, and David Steel, leader of the Liberal Democrats, came to inflate Ceauşescu's ego over a very short space of time. I was Chargé d'Affaires when the lady came, and I met her at the airport where, typically, her baggage failed to accompany her on the British Airways flight. Embassy wives rallied round and produced enough spares to keep her going until her suitcase turned up, but she was far from happy, though it did not show when she posed for the usual stomach-churning, smiling photographs with Ceauşescu. The homilies they exchanged, praising each other to the skies, are better left buried in the soil-pit of history.

During the Wilson visit mentioned earlier, complex negotiations took place with the Romanians over their bid to buy thirteen BAC1 11 aircraft from Britain. All British companies needed slush funds to do business in Romania, but even those hard-nosed aircraft company executives were startled when at the eleventh hour – actually shortly before midnight – the Romanians said yes, they agreed to the terms of the contract, provided that BAC, as part of the deal, also bought from them £150,000 worth of gent's ready-made suiting and £30,000 worth of tinned tomatoes, and repaired the roof of the Romanian Orthodox Church in London. The BAC delegation, with the British government officials looking away and pretending they didn't hear, briefly demurred, then caved in. It was part of the Romanian way of life.

It was a time and a place for spies and counterspies. I knew several of them, declared or undeclared, from several different countries. It was always a bit of a game for us straight diplomats to see, for example, how long it took to spot the CIA man at the American Embassy. We usually got there in the end, despite their professionalism (though the wife of one of them behaved with a distinct lack of discipline when she tried to smuggle her Romanian lover out of the country in the boot of her car, helped by its supposedly inviolate diplomatic number-plates). I still have the brief obituary of one British spy I knew. He would have been amused by one sentence, which read: 'He had a successful career, in the course of which he generally succeeded in concealing the ability, hard work and dedication which he brought to his chosen profession.'

Friendly Romanians told us that they presumed all British diplomats were spies of one sort or another and I suppose we were.

I built up a particular relationship with Romania because several of the spy thrillers I had written were translated into Romanian, and I received the royalties from them, thus allowing me to save my Foreign Office pay back in London. That may sound like a simple transaction, but in fact it was far from it. First of all, the Foreign Office itself was keen to ensure that there was absolutely no possibility of my being bribed or suborned by the deal I had with my Romanian publishing house. Secondly, my books had always been subject to vetting by the Office: indeed, my using the pen name Michael Sinclair for my first six books was result of them urging anonymity on me. Since my first thriller was set in Bonn while I was a diplomat there, it could conceivably have led to difficulties, as I had inserted various German spies and counterspies, both good and bad, into my plot.

In Romania, however, things went a step further, and my manuscripts were threatened with a certain amount of 'revisionism'. I refused to have any cuts made, but I did allow the translators to disperse certain footnotes throughout the text. For example, in one of my books, I had Adolf Hitler escaping to South America, and living there in safety until sometime in the mid-sixties. Since the communist authorities were always worried about a resurgence of fascism, the footnote firmly proclaims that the book is absolutely and completely fictional, and that there was no shred of reliable evidence that Hitler had ever escaped from his Berlin bunker.

Where better, when talking of spies, to mention one particular traitor who was an ancient relic of the Cold War. As Press Secretary at Buckingham Palace I had to handle the public revelation of the treachery of Sir Anthony Blunt, The Queen's former Surveyor of Paintings. To put this story in context, when the Peter Wright *Spycatcher* story broke, it conjured up memories of security lectures I had attended on first joining the Foreign Office, which always referred to the Burgess, Maclean and Philby betrayals. In the Cabinet Office, it was difficult not to have been hooked by dubious stories of right-wing plots, orchestrated, according to Wright, by up to thirty members of the Security Service, or MI5, to overthrow

Prime Minister Harold Wilson. Then there were the rumours concerning the newspaper baron Cecil King, who was accused of attempting to enlist Lord Mountbatten in 'bringing sense to the British people'. The 'wilderness of mirrors' which is espionage, to paraphrase Wright, is a place where 'defectors are false, lies are truth, truth lies, and the reflections leave you dazzled and confused'.

Some years later, when I was working for Lord Hanson, Alan Bennett asked if he could come to see me. He had written a play, *A Question of Attribution*, principally about Blunt, but with The Queen as the other main character. Would the system allow Her Majesty to be portrayed on stage? I gave a personal view: so much would depend on how well it was done. In the event the play was a stunning success. The portrayal of the monarch closely questioning the spy demonstrated only too well the cool percipience of the real person. When Princess Margaret saw Prunella Scales playing her sister, she praised the acting to the skies, right down to all the little touches of voice and handbag.

Many of those involved in real-life espionage are larger than life figures in their own right, doing deeds and suborning others in ways that challenge the most inventive of authors. This has been a recurring problem throughout my thriller-writing career; there is always a huge competition between the best fiction and the exciting reality of international diplomatic life.

The efficient management of perception is the first rule of diplomacy. The second is that experience has to run counter to expectation in order to call it experience. My generation were all ideologists in those early days, and experience was yet to come. We demonstrated against things and for things. We believed passionately in this or that. Things – not just environmental, green, friendly things – mattered to us, like nuclear disarmament, the rights of oppressed peoples everywhere, and the relics of colonialism and neo-colonialism, an expression that has gone out of fashion, or has been redefined as globalisation. In the sixties, the mainstream political parties were diametrically opposed on a range of fundamental matters. Today they pretend to disagree with each other, but real differences scarcely exist. Idealism fades where consensus politics rules. Past ideologies are laid waste, and their elderly protagonists in their eventide homes watch bleakly as the skies darken with their once politically correct chickens coming home to roost.

In those far-off days, when 'Government Property' was still stamped on every sheet of official lavatory paper, I remember heavy arguments with other young diplomats on ideological matters, and the interaction of these arguments with practical politics. The first night I took my future wife out I made the dangerous decision of inviting her to a dinner along with two friends, Hugh Stephenson, later editor of the *New Statesman* and then Professor of Journalism at the City University, and Peter Jay, a Treasury official, who became British Ambassador to Washington and a distinguished BBC correspondent. The intellectual level was high, if arcane. When he was economics editor of *The Times*, Peter once received a complaint from one of his sub-editors to the effect that he couldn't understand a word of the article that he had just been given.

'You're not meant to', came Peter's brisk reply. 'It's written for three people: two at the Treasury and one at the Bank of England.'

The only story I can offer about Hugh relates to a later occasion, when I was at the Palace and he was editor of the *New Statesman*, a publication not renowned for its overwhelming support for the Monarchy. He did admit, however, that, following Diana's engagement, when he daringly put her picture on the front cover of the magazine, he almost doubled his modest circulation figures. I rang him from the Palace one day, and the *New Statesman* operator asked for my name and from where I was calling. When I told her, there was a stunned silence then a shriek of excitement, and eventually Hugh came on with a fierce, 'Didn't I tell you never to ring me at the office!'

Conversation over dinner that first evening almost finished my relationship with my Norwegian and, as yet, not terribly good-at-speaking-English, wife-to-be, Mona. The conversation, as she clearly remembers it, revolved entirely round someone who was never explained to her, called George. He had huge attributes and major defects. George was an alcoholic. George was brilliant before six o'clock in the evening. George was a visionary. George could solve the Middle East problems single-handed, because he knew Golda so well. George could do this. George could do that. George was a failure through and through. Who the hell was George?

George was George Brown, one of the most gifted failures in postwar British political life. Drink was his problem and drink, when he was Foreign Secretary, finished him. For all his failings, he was great at quick repartee, particularly at the height of President de Gaulle's vendetta against Britain and her entry to the European Common Market. I remember first meeting him at a party at the house of his nephew, Norman Hackett, who introduced me as a member of the Foreign Office. I wore, unusually for the British Diplomatic Service at the time, a long beard. 'Which Foreign Office? Surely not ours?' Brown asked. He had a point. I had grown a beard at university, but shaved it off, as I was recommended to do, before sitting the Foreign Service entry competition. My adviser, a former ambassador, had told me that anyone in the service was allowed one small eccentricity. The trouble was that I was using mine up in that hirsute way: what would happen if the selection panel discovered others? On entry, I grew it again immediately.

Continuing with the theme of hair, de Gaulle's anti-British policies were obviously weighing on George Brown's mind at the party. Sipping furiously from a glass of orange juice, he joked that the French were effective in only one respect: they had invented an extreme measure for curing dandruff. It was known as the guillotine.

In the Embassy in Bonn when this French attitude was at its most robust, we mocked their policies with schoolboy wit, particularly in our annual Christmas revue, the social highlight of the year. We had a number of very talented scriptwriters on the staff, who just managed to avoid causing major diplomatic offence – we had to, since many Germans and diplomats from other embassies were in the audience. One little number reflected on de Gaulle's veto, and, to the tune of 'We are two little sheep who have gone astray', went as follows:

To the booming lands of Europe,
To the place where Charlie dwells,
Come the Anglo-Saxon masses all aglee,
With the problems of our Sterling, and our Agriculture too,
And our hang-ups about he-ge-mon-y.

CHORUS
Gentlemen diplomats all are we,
Come to plead on bended knee,
Charlie, have mercy on such as we.
Non! Non! Non!

We later had evidence that the French studiously reported this frivolity to the Quai d'Orsay in Paris. How could the Brits make light of such a serious subject?

Stories about George Brown were legion, and most, like him in his cups mistaking the papal nuncio in his purple robes for a woman and asking him to dance, are more legendary than true. But one legend is true: he received one ambassador, whom he thought was Swedish, and lectured the poor man on his government's disgraceful attitude towards American policy in Vietnam. After ten minutes of this tirade, the visitor tried to interrupt with, 'But, Foreign Secretary, I am not the Swedish Ambassador to the Court of St James. I'm the British Ambassador to Stockholm.'

'So?' came the brusque reply. 'Doesn't matter. You people are all the same.'

As President of the Liberal students at Edinburgh University, my previous political connections had been with that party, and, in particular, with David Steel and Jo Grimond. Jo, a true idealist, would send me telegrams – yes, telegrams – of the old type, white paper tape laboriously stuck to little forms. He asked for my advice, not just to do with student politics, but on South Africa, Rhodesian sanctions, or Scottish affairs. I was flattered. I would send him long dispatches, which he claimed he was grateful for. Grimond was one of the last of the old school, the aristocratic member for Orkney and Shetland, with a strong belief in certain values, and an elegant charm to go with it, which few among subsequent generations of political leaders in Britain have come anywhere close to emulating. Grimond's policies had recruited David Steel, first as a Liberal candidate, then as the youngest ever MP, and he tried to induce me, too, to stand for an Edinburgh seat. I declined. I have no regrets on that score, but I did have increasing regrets about the gradual death of my convictions.

FIVE

Establishment Rules

Quick! Hire a teenager while they still have all the answers.

Anon.

When we left university and became junior civil servants or diplomats, we still believed in things. There was an informal club of young diplomats working in Downing Street, who had, in our student days, demonstrated outside Number 10 on various issues. It was easier then. There were no huge gates at the end of the street, and demonstrators could come right up to the prime minister's front door, where, I remember, a solitary figure, an old man in a beret (and, when the weather was bad, a huge umbrella to cover him) would kneel on the pavement outside the door and pray every single morning of the year. I am grateful to Jeremy Paxman for reminding me that the dominance of Oxbridge candidates entering the Foreign Service was still overwhelming, and that when I was recruited in 1963, I was the first graduate from a Scottish university to have been selected in eight years, and one of only three not to have come from Oxford or Cambridge.

The skills required were unspoken. Again, perception ruled. Harold Nicolson defined them clearly when he wrote:

These then are the qualities of my ideal diplomatist: truth, accuracy, calm, patience, good temper, modesty and loyalty. They are also the qualities of an ideal diplomacy. 'But', the reader may object, 'you have forgotten intelligence, discernment, prudence, hospitality, charm, industry, courage and even tact.' I have not forgotten them. I have taken them for granted.

Such glittering expectations of diplomacy were firmly brought down to earth immediately on entering the Foreign Office, that grand building designed by Sir Gilbert Scott and completed in all its magnificence in 1868. Its role had grown much since then, the gilded rooms and staircases dangerously neglected, built in and around with holes knocked through walls, and desks for junior recruits like me even inserted into huge Victorian fireplaces where soot from long past fires would regularly drop down and blacken the most carefully polished dispatch from some far-flung corner of the globe. Windows were seldom cleaned, the furniture should have been thrown out years ago, and there was always the sound of building and making-do, clipping on chipboard hutches in the Durbar Courtyard and to the very roofs of that once great building, making it a shabby rabbit warren, which surely had its effect not just on our morale, but on British foreign policy itself.

The Foreign Office in those days was a department of state where 'process' ruled. Drafts of submissions to ministers seemed largely directed at stopping them taking initiatives of their own, which would undoubtedly be antipathetic to British interests, at least in the eyes of the Foreign Office mandarins. Draft telegrams to overseas posts were polished to perfection before they were dispatched. The German Foreign Office in Bonn had been much the same: it too believed in the *Schönheitsbericht* – the beautiful report. Handling ministers with gilded words was more important than handling overseas relations. I was lectured thus by one of my heads of department, a man who, to me, seemed to have a difficulty for every solution. I can still remember, when dealing with the Middle Eastern dispute, and a hijacking by the girl terrorist Laila Khaled, that he sat agonising over my emergency telegram of guidance to our embassy in Tel Aviv, changing 'buts' to 'ands' and back again, 'for we must get the resonance right'.

We are all fascinated by long-buried secrets – witness the John Major–Edwina Currie affair – and I sometimes grow a little concerned that, under the thirty-year rule covering the release of government papers, some of my elementary advice to my superiors on the problems of the Middle East will one day be subjected to contemporary scrutiny.

Some friends argue that the death of our ideology came with the Wilson government. Some believe it has never died. Wilson certainly was an opportunist, but his supporters insist that expediency is not always wrong. Privately, for example, we now know that Wilson and the British government had no time for Ceauşescu, or what he stood for, but that had not stopped him, during that visit to Bucharest in September 1975, addressing the communist dictator in the following terms:

. . . Mr President . . . Our talks today were for me particularly interesting and instructive, and at the end of them I told my colleagues on the British delegation that rarely, in many years of diplomatic contacts, have I had such an important conversation or have I met such valuable views as yours on numerous questions . . . Thus, once again, it confirms my view – and I think I was right to say this to my colleagues at the end of today's talks – that I can recall only two or three people in the world who possess such a vision as yours, such an understanding of the matters over which we have ranged this evening. As a matter of fact I compared you with Aneurin Bevan, who had this special ability to see the wood for the trees, to see the whole in detail. And I think that this similarity does not stop here.

Wilson's loyal and affectionate wife, Mary, who was much mocked when it was discovered that she wrote poetry (the media would doubtless still mock wives of prime ministers today for writing poetry), appeared to be left to one side, for we always saw him surrounded by more possessive women, in particular Marcia Williams, later Lady Falkender, and Barbara Castle, both of whom were, for all their attributes, heartily disliked, at least by most of the media. Doubtless with the subtle help of the Number 10 Press Secretary, Joe Haines, the political correspondents interpreted Marcia Williams's influence on Wilson as being almost entirely perverse, as subsequent memoirs have confirmed, so no change there in terms of an inherent dislike of kitchen cabinets. Her notorious 'Lavender List' of recommended honours, on Wilson's unexpected resignation as Prime Minister in May 1976, included some of the most unlikely names ever put forward for an award in the second half of the twentieth century. Submission of that list prompted The Queen's then Private Secretary to ring Downing Street to ask if the Prime Minister was being serious with his proposals, only to be told that he was.

There was one exception to the media's dislike of Marcia Williams, as I had gradually become aware during my time in Bonn. I met frequently with the *Daily Mail*'s well-liked political correspondent, Walter Terry, who seemed to get a lot of privileged access, particularly when Harold Wilson and George Brown swept through on their tour of Europe, on a mission to try to defeat de Gaulle's veto on British entry to the Common Market. Terry always seemed exceptionally well informed about British politics as well as current German attitudes to the issues, and I said as much in one lengthy economic report to my Ambassador, Sir Frank Roberts.

His deputy summoned me the next day. 'H.E. doesn't like talking about such things, but are you seeing more of Walter Terry?'

'Yes,' I said. 'We're having a drink together tonight.'

'Careful!' I was told. *Careful*? In those days that was some warning. The Cold War was at its height. Was he perhaps a spy, or likely to leak sensitive information in the wrong direction?

My superior smiled. 'Head in the clouds, Shea. He's, how shall I put it, a close friend, very, of Marcia Williams, Harold's right-hand woman, his political and private secretary.'

It was only later that the affair between them became public knowledge. In those days such things were seldom reported on, particularly by a subservient press, where access to Number 10, and the prime minister, was controlled by that gatekeeper of gatekeepers, Marcia herself. And to think how we had all smiled at the current *Private Eye* joke, 'Why does Harold Wilson have his hand on Barbara Castle's knee?' Answer: 'To keep his mind off sex.' We smiled again when Marcia became Lady Falkender.

Sex has always been the ladder to success for some, and the trapdoor to failure for others. Think of Bill Clinton or Gary Hart, who memorably said of a certain Miss Donna Rice, that 'sex was not part of our relationship'. Who is ever going to believe remarks like that again? The singer, Madonna, on the other hand, has admitted that 'losing my virginity was a career move', but such honest claims are rare, since trapdoors are much more appealing to the tabloid segments of our minds. We can usually bear with equanimity the misfortunes of others, particularly those we dislike, and I have come across a few of those too. When the private side of life lets a career down, a careful choice of words is handy. Had I been advising the Chairman of the Conservative Party, Cecil Parkinson, as his reputation manager, I might have suggested a more thoughtful expression than his talking about 'my little indiscretion', to describe his illegitimate child when he met people at parties.

On the subject of sex, a frequent visitor to our house in Lambeth in earlier days was Jeremy Thorpe, then Leader of the Liberals in the House of Commons. He came with David Steel, and, from my experience, it was difficult to give any credence to the accusations made against him by Norman Scott, given Jeremy's apparently highly heterosexual interest in the attractive Norwegian au pair girls we had at the time. When, eventually, he had to resign in 1976, the Party lost a hugely entertaining man with a rapier wit.

Ideology did not end with Harold Wilson. It had ended a long time before that. But one thing any senior diplomat or civil servant learns early on, is that no matter what political party is in power, and while British politicians may sing the same broken old songs, they are, by and large, not lining their own pockets financially in the process. Nevertheless, expediency and opportunism have always ruled. And no amount of spindoctoring, though it was called by other terms in those days, could prevent the media having a go. It is not always the main player's fault. At one exclusive lunch, I found myself sitting beside Freddy Laker, who helped usher in the era of cheap transatlantic flights for us poor travellers. He was in the middle of a massive fight against the major airlines, but he spoke only of a coruscating battle he was having with his former wife over the custody of his child. The media attention given to the latter had taken the guts out of him in dealing with the airlines. You cannot fight a public and a private battle at the same time, if the media are waiting for your fall.

Without realising it, when I joined the Diplomatic Service I had stepped on the first rung of the Establishment ladder, where 'being suitable' was the most British of all character judgements. Whether the Establishment, defined as the matrix of the great and the good, exists, or did exist, has long been debated, ever since Henry Fairlie first wrote about it in the *Spectator* in the mid-fifties. It remains, to my mind, a determinant of how the British ruling class always works, emerging as it did from the class-stratified 'old boy network', to evolve into today's equally compelling 'system' of getting one's way by dint of who one knows.

By and large, those who were 'in' the Establishment, by being members of an unstructured group of power-brokers from politics, business and the professions, tended to deny its very existence. Those outside it believed it did exist, and that it still does. They know this, quite simply, because things keep happening, decisions get taken, and people get appointed to the 'right' positions through a mechanism that is separate from the publicly established and acknowledged ways of taking decisions that affect the public at large. My ageing copy of the *Oxford English Dictionary* adds that the Establishment achieves its effect 'by virtue of its traditional superiority, and the use especially of a tacit understanding, a common mode of speech, and having a general interest in the maintenance of the status quo'. It does not just happen in Britain. The film director David, now Lord, Puttnam recalled that when he went off to Hollywood, the battles with the closely protective 'people-system' he found and was obliged to fight, allowed him no time to produce films.

No matter how government spindoctors may try to market modern aspirations about accountability and openness, experience sells things differently. I was in a West End club the night before I wrote these words, and I listened in on a conversation between three members of the great and good, though not one of them currently held a senior political position. They were deciding on who was to be appointed to a major public office. And, yes, their first choice as Chairman of the BBC was duly selected. Yes, London's clubs are still the source of knowing much of what is going on, what currently matters in political life, and who is going to get what job. The Australian lawyer, Malcolm Turnbull, who fought the British Establishment over the *Spycatcher* case and encouraged the then Cabinet Secretary, Robert Armstrong, to use his most memorable quote about being 'economical with the truth', has recorded that he picked up a huge amount of gossip at the Garrick about that particular case, merely by listening to what the Attorney General, Sir Nigel Havers, talked loudly and openly about to all who were present. I believe it, since I once had to remonstrate with that Law Lord when I sat with him over a table, and he started regaling everyone within earshot about the sensitive misdeeds of a junior royal, which resulted in us putting an injunction on a would-be salacious story appearing in the tabloids. Armstrong's successor, Robin Butler, made the same point as his predecessor about flirtations with honesty, though without garnering so many headlines, when in his evidence to the Scott Report he said, 'You do not give all the information that is available to you. By doing that, it does not follow that you mislead people. . . . Half the picture can be true'. How half true that is!

Having sat in on dozens of meetings or appointment boards in my time, I have seen that 'suitability' or 'the right sort of background' –

rather like being in Mrs Thatcher's 'one of us' category – won out over the best CV, or the best quality of strategy or applicant. Enoch Powell talked about the process as being 'the power that need not speak its name', which is an apt enough description of the way Establishment members just 'know', in any given set of circumstances, what is a correct decision, and what an unsafe one.

In the past, the leading figures in the law, the Church, academia and the professions were seen as right-wing allies of the wider Conservative Party. No longer: such key individuals ally themselves as best they can to whatever party, or wing of a party, is in power. In this lies their strength, their flexibility and their skill. They will never have heard of him, but they all ape that astute man, the first Earl of Lauderdale, who wrote in 1670, 'success equals being a willow when others are oaks'. The members of today's Establishment, and they are still mainly male, are men for all seasons, knowing, above all, who is in and who is out.

The Scottish mafia is a particularly adept part of that nebulous but coherent system, both inside Scotland and also in Westminster and Whitehall. They may not be members of London's key clubs, though many are, but they know each other's weaknesses, and, consequently, how to get things done. Scots have long had a hugely disproportionate place and say in the running of the United Kingdom as a whole, for they are a clever fraternity of interlocking circles of influence. Eat with them, drink with them, hear how they talk, and, if you are a fellow Scot, you know instantly where you are with them, and how you can play them. They have subtle ways of allowing those who show their worth to join their club on probation, but it is a club with 'understood' rather than written rules.

Among the best of the older generation of that mafia was Scotland's first First Minister, Donald Dewar. Having debated against him in our student days, he from Glasgow University, I from Edinburgh, I had long been a fan. There was a memorable evening when David Steel gave a dinner for the leaders of the four Scottish parties on the night of the opening of the first Scottish Parliament in

300 years. No secrets, but the mood was tense at the beginning of the evening, though by the time I was invited to join them for a nightcap, Scotland's amber nectar and Dewar's wit had well mellowed the proceedings.

Better still was a lunch in the Great Hall at Edinburgh Castle, hosted by Dewar for The Queen of Denmark. He had her in fits of laughter with his stories, even commenting on the politically incorrect fur coat that remained draped around her shoulders throughout the lunch. But roles were reversed, and even he was silenced for a moment when she leant across to him at the end of the meal, and, in a monarchical voice, asked him if he minded if she smoked.

For all his skills and political nous, Dewar was naïve when it came to some of the little things of life. When he became First Minister, his staff had to bully him into buying an overcoat, and he had no interest in the mundane, like cars. At the very last Party Political Conference of the Labour Party he attended, he found he was running late for his next appointment. There was no official car available, so a kindly businessman friend offered him his very expensive car and chauffeur to take him to his destination. On arrival, Donald opened the heavy door in a hurry, and smashed it into the side of a passing taxi. Hugely embarrassed, he pressed a £10 note into the chauffeur's hand, and told him to get it fixed. The damaged door was repaired, and nobody could bring themselves to tell Donald how many thousands of pounds it had actually cost.

In the old days in the Civil or Foreign Service, cars did not come into it. You knew your rank by the size of your desk, your office, and whether you had carpet or linoleum on the floor. When I worked at the Cabinet Office, the then Secretary to the Cabinet, Sir Burke Trend, may have had an official car, but we used to pass him in the evenings, waiting in the rain for a number eleven bus in Whitehall. Was it a mere week after the Falklands were invaded that I saw, newly resigned from the great office of Foreign Secretary, Lord Carrington waiting for a tube in Westminster underground station? Perhaps this gives us a fuller understanding of Malcolm

Rifkind's response, shortly after he himself had lost office, also as Foreign Secretary, to the journalist who asked what his daily routine was now like.

'Oh it's much the same,' said Malcolm. 'I get up, shave, dress, have breakfast with my wife, pick up my briefcase, go out and jump into the back of my car . . . and it doesn't go anywhere.'

Back to the sixties. In those death-throes of ideology, who suffered worst at the hands of the press, Harold Wilson or Alec Douglas-Home? The latter certainly had a hard time, and he never seemed to have any spindoctors around him. When he first stood for the House of Commons as Lord Dunglass, my grandfather, a Lanarkshire mill owner, chaired his adoption meeting. My mother recalled her despairing father coming home, bewailing, as a result of an incredibly hesitant and badly delivered speech by the candidate, that the 'pair wee laddie will ne'er get anywhere'. But Sir Alec became prime minister in the end, as did the much-mocked Clement Attlee, who wrote in short defence of his own career:

> *Few thought he was even a starter*
> *There were many who thought themselves smarter,*
> *But he ended P.M.*
> *C.H. and O.M.*
> *An Earl and a Knight of the Garter.*

Attlee was a wise bird, who realised that the powerful influence the powerful. When, in his June 1945 electioneering, Churchill suggested that a vote for Labour might usher in a new Gestapo, he famously responded, 'The voice was the voice of Churchill, but the mind was the mind of Beaverbrook.' Of himself, however, he modestly admitted, 'I have none of the qualities that create publicity.' How might he have survived in this new media age?

In the sixties' 'Establishment Club' era of political satire, *Private Eye* and the television programme *That Was The Week That Was*, both devastatingly clever, mocked the whole British power base. They had a huge effect on the ability of politicians to survive. The home secretary of the day, whom I was briefly seconded to work for, Henry Brooke, was always referred to in *Private Eye* as 'Poor Old Henry Brooke', which did nothing for his morale any more than did the various jokes about Harold Wilson and his pragmatism, as in the jibe, 'The two worst things about Harold are his face!'

For some years in the mid-sixties, as a so-called Resident Clerk at the Foreign Office, I was one of four or five young diplomats who had a flat at the top of the Foreign Office building, to look after the affairs of state overnight. We had to deal with urgent telegrams that flooded in from our Embassies and High Commissions around the world. We were young, but for a brief time we were allowed this broader view of the world's problems as they affected the United Kingdom, something we would not have an opportunity to enjoy again until we were very senior. One night, David Steel, by then a young Liberal MP, came to visit me in my roof-top rooms. In those less secure days, girlfriends could come to visit us, and because of the splendour of our accommodation, we got few rejections when inviting dates to 'come back for a nightcap'. The security officers in those pre-IRA days used to sign them in as 'cousins', particularly if they spent the night there, a happy euphemism for such unlikely threats to the nation's security. But that evening, David had in tow his friend Judith Todd, the daughter of Garfield Todd, Prime Minister of Southern Rhodesia from 1953 until 1958. No harm in that either, except that both the carpet of my room and my desk were covered in red boxes of secret telegrams and files dealing with the Rhodesian crisis.

Our most difficult task always seemed to be whether to wake a senior official or a minister in the middle of the night to tell them some piece of startling news. I was on duty when Rhodesia eventually declared UDI, and I recall having to wake the Foreign Secretary, as I had been instructed to do, when the news finally came through that Ian Smith had made his breakaway attempt. On 11 November 1965, probably before almost anyone in the United Kingdom, I saw the text of his speech.

'We have struck a blow,' Smith said, 'for the preservation of justice, civilisation and Christianity; and in the spirit of this belief, we have this day assumed our sovereign independence.'

How the world condemned him, as they condemn today's evil aftermath in poor Zimbabwe!

As Resident Clerks we also had to deal with ministers, particularly Conservative ministers, when they had finished dining at their clubs. Not just they, but a surprising number of members of other parties would decide to handle complicated issues when somewhat tired and emotional. Late one night, Rab Butler rang to have what turned out to be quite a long chat with me, an unknown junior Foreign Service diplomat. He needed someone to talk to. He poured out his woes. Indecision was the key word as far as Mr Butler was concerned that night, and on the back of that experience and little else, it was probably right that The Queen chose Macmillan instead as prime minister in 1957. I noted down somewhere that Mr Butler told me, 'no politician in his right mind keeps an open one', but he certainly did, to the bitter end, which was doubtless also why he never reached the top of the tree. When he left office he complained that, removed from the circulation list of Foreign Office telegrams, he would now, to his chagrin, have to read the daily newspapers once again.

Prime ministers and foreign secretaries would ring up Resident Clerks at odd hours. The trouble was that one's friends would get rather good at pretending to be prime ministers or foreign secretaries too, and one was never quite sure, when a voice said, 'Prime Minister here', whether it was Sir Alec Douglas-Home or some clever mimic. On one occasion we held a Resident Clerks' Ball, a glittering black-tie occasion, which went well except that in the middle of the night my fellow Resident Clerk, David Wilson, now Lord Wilson, and a former Governor of Hong Kong, decided to play the bagpipes on the roof of the Foreign Office. We received a phone call from someone who actually turned out to be Sir Alec, the Prime Minister, saying that he did not much mind anyone playing the pipes and waking up everyone in Central London, but would the piper please tune his drones.

As a young diplomat in the late sixties, one of my most memorable trips was as bag-carrier and scribe to Tony Parsons, my Under-Secretary for Middle Eastern Affairs, who was later to become Ambassador to the United Nations. We flew to Washington for talks with Henry Kissinger, who had been appointed National Security Adviser to Nixon in 1969, four years before he became American Secretary of State. Over the two or three times I met him, I gained the impression that he was a man, like Talleyrand, who hoarded clever quotes to impress his guests for maximum effect. It worked. Having been in Bonn and having heard Willi Brandt talk in his slightly accented English, here we had an American statesman whose deep guttural tones became world famous. When Nixon met the Israeli Prime Minister Golda Meir, he said to her something to the effect that Israel and the US now both had Jewish Foreign Ministers.

'Yes', Mrs Meir responded, 'but mine speaks English.'

Kissinger boldly expressed his criticisms of some British diplomats. He wrote, 'The British capitalise on their accent when they don't want you to know what they are saying. But if you wake them up at 4 a.m., they speak perfect English, the same damn way as we do.' He was referring to the euphemisms that are still part of the lingua franca of much diplomatic parlance. Some of it seems designed to confuse, but most of the French expressions, such as *chargé d'affaires*, or *attaché* or *aide-mémoire*, in diplomat-speak are relics of an age when their use was designed to help communication between peoples. Lord Chalfont, the distinguished statesman and former Foreign Office minister, has said about diplomatic communication that it was always 'lucidly presented, persuasively argued, and formidably monolithic'. He continued: 'Dissent and reservation is carefully ironed out at official level; what is presented to the minister is the considered, agreed Foreign Office view. If he is disobliging enough to reject it, the process has to begin again; and in case ministers should disrupt the machine by trying to initiate policies themselves, they are kept busy with an endless stream of telegrams, despatches, cabinet papers, parliamentary questions and miscellaneous correspondence.'

The Office was, and doubtless still is, outstanding in appearing to offer ministers a choice, but not all the options were equal, and the official line was almost invariably taken in the end, for, as always, presentation of the argument was king.

Back to Kissinger. At our meetings, at which I was the note-taker, he began by explaining to Tony Parsons that while in his present position he took a great deal of interest in the Middle East, he would never ever consider getting involved publicly, precisely because he was Jewish. Some hope. He had the knack of reconciling the irreconcilable, as he did in his brokering of the US North Vietnam ceasefire, which won him the Nobel Peace Prize. He even escaped being sullied by his close relationship with Nixon, and came as close as anyone to bringing about peace in the Middle East. That first day we met him, however, he was full of clever quotes, not all of them fully meaningful, such as, 'If you want things to stay the same, then things have to change.' They sounded impressive at the time, although when I came to produce a record of the meeting, which was the only reason I was present, their substance was more than a little thin.

I wrote down another quote from Kissinger, though this one he generously attributed to Dean Acheson, 'No memorandum is written to inform the reader, but to protect the writer.' The man who stated, 'I don't give a damn for protocol. I'm a swinger. Bring on the beautiful spies', also told us the story of a meeting he had just had with Foreign Minister Gromyko, his opposite number in Moscow. To underline the fact that he knew the Russians were bugging all the rooms the Americans had had allocated to them, as he sat across the green baize table from his Soviet counterpart, he held a briefing paper above his head in the direction of the chandeliers and said 'Two copies please'. Some of his remarks were seriously funny. Another I recall was that the main advantage of being famous, apart from its being a great aphrodisiac, was that when you bored people, they thought it was all their fault.

Kissinger, as always, came up with a most telling argument on the limitations of trying to create a believable political identity. Writing later about the fall of Nixon, he wrote:

> To have striven so hard, to have moulded a public personality out of so amorphous an identity . . . only to end with every weakness disclosed . . . was a fate of biblical proportions. Evidently the Deity would not tolerate the presumption that all could be manipulated.

My boss, Tony Parsons, was the man who, long before the TV programme *Yes, Minister*, again took me with him, as record-taker, this time to see Foreign Secretary George Brown about some new initiative the latter had thought up for solving the Middle Eastern dispute. Brown, as was said earlier, was both gifted and flawed. He had a Jewish wife, and he thought he knew all Israel's problems backwards, but he let himself down badly, doubtless in his cups, when he referred to the Israeli Prime Minister Golda Meir as 'just an old Russian Babushka'. It caused a huge flurry of criticism behind the scenes.

On this particular occasion the Foreign Secretary defined his Arab-Israel initiative, then waited for Parsons' considered response.

'My goodness, that would be a most courageous decision for you to take, Foreign Secretary', the latter said, in best diplomat-speak.

'Courageous?' End of initiative.

Another Middle Eastern memory revolves around my sitting in a small executive jet, waiting for a future prime minister to return. It was 1971. I was the desk officer dealing with the Arab–Israel dispute, and, because of financial stringencies, I was also, absurdly, the only member of my Foreign Office department who had never been to the Middle East. Thus, when my departmental head heard that the then Minister of Education, one Margaret Thatcher, a largely unknown figure at the time, was flying out to Jerusalem in a private plane, he arranged for me to be given a lift, thereby allowing me two brief days of experience of Israel and the Israelis. That visit is a story for another time, except that I ended up on my second night there in the company of the British Consul-General in Jerusalem, sitting at a table with almost the most important figure in Israel at the time, the legendary one-eyed Moshe Dayan, currently their Minister of Defence. He wore his distinctive piratical black eyepiece, but I remember particularly how small and tubby he was, wrapped up in a sort of battledress, pulled in at the middle by a soldier's belt, and, even though we were in a restaurant, he was wearing a very tired-looking black beret that failed to hide the snowstorm of dandruff around his shoulders. But did he sparkle! I could have listened to him all night long.

The trip itself was remarkable in a number of ways. First of all, as we flew out of Northolt, the Minister, who sat opposite me in the cramped HS 125 with her overawed Private Secretary beside her, was most concerned at reading in that morning's papers about the student demonstrations that had taken place over the previous weekend, condemning her decision to do away with free school milk and calling her 'Thatcher – the milk snatcher'. The outcry greatly upset her, and she kept saying so.

There were only three of us in the cabin, and two pilots, so I had plenty of time to talk to Mrs Thatcher and get to know her. Even then she had a darting quality about her, walking about with very short steps, or swivelling round to look at you. She was forever busy, a little shrill, but never lacking in the conviction of her prejudices. I also remember a sympathetic and pleasant lady, though with a voice that was a part octave higher and several decibels more strident than it was later trained to become. She spent much of the journey doing her air-stewardess bit, making sure that her Private Secretary and I were well fed with the sandwiches that someone had thoughtfully provided. It was on that occasion I first heard her remark, demonstrating her well-ordered mind, that 'a ticked-off list of chores was pure happiness'.

The HS 125 plane was small, and we had to refuel, both going out and coming home. On the way out to Israel there were no problems, but coming home the pilot, for his own reasons, decided that we would refuel at a civilian airfield he knew well on a Greek island. What the pilot had failed to take into account was that since his last visit, there had been a military coup, led by the notorious Greek Colonels. His chosen airport was now a heavily guarded military base, and so, when we were forced to land, explaining that we were running out of fuel, our little plane was immediately surrounded by a large number of soldiers, wielding an imposing range of machine-guns. If we were mistaken for some hostile invasion force, we were an insignificant one. Nonetheless, the pilot appeared in the cabin to explain rather sheepishly to the Minister that we were ordered to go and explain ourselves to the Colonel Commandant of the airfield. Ungallantly and unceremoniously, we males decided that the Minister of Education was by far the best person to deal with the natives. We remained on board, the Private Secretary, the shamefaced pilot, and the ashen-faced Michael Shea. We peered through the windows as Mrs Thatcher was marched off on her high heels towards the nearest barracks.

The political life of the United Kingdom might have been rather different two decades later if Mrs Thatcher had not shown that she was made of sterner stuff. We waited for a long, nervous hour, then she reappeared bearing a huge basket full of oranges, and we were waved on our way back to Britain by a bunch of smiling Greek soldiers. The lady tells the story rather differently.

Who was the most overlooked of foreign secretaries? Probably the long-forgotten Michael Stewart, a modest man with, as has been said of others, much to be modest about, but he was a great respecter of us junior diplomats and we liked him for that. Some Foreign Office mandarins mocked Stewart's gentle style, and he wrote later that 'It was a Foreign Office joke that I could never make a speech of any length without using the word "mankind": it seems to me a good word for a Foreign Secretary to have firmly fixed in his head.' There are many such buzzwords of the peace and motherhood variety used in diplomacy all the time, though it was always better to recognise the realities of international affairs and the cynicism of journalists before doing what the New Labour government did when first elected in 1997, with its much blazoned 'Ethical Foreign Policy'. But Robin Cook was Foreign Secretary by that time, and the media went for him in a big way over this. Cook would never have been chosen by Hollywood had they been making a film about the British Diplomatic Service: the perception of leadership is all important in world affairs, and Britain has been badly served of late in that regard.

Working at the Foreign Office, or in the Cabinet Office, to which I was seconded for two years in the early seventies, even fairly junior members of staff saw something of the prime ministers and the foreign secretaries of the day, including, in my case, Jim Callaghan and Edward Heath. Callaghan, a competent foreign secretary, was forthright in saying how much he valued his private audiences with The Queen, since his respect for her well preceded his time as prime minister. While he was still Foreign Secretary, he recorded in his book *Time and Chance* that in 1976 she had encouraged him to keep talking to Ian Smith, even after the Rhodesians had declared unilateral independence. When, in 1977, Callaghan, then prime minister, presented The Queen with a silver coffee pot to mark her Silver Jubilee, The Queen, in thanking him, said that she knew that on a similar occasion in the nineteenth century Lord Salisbury had given Queen Victoria a present of a portrait of himself. 'Thank you for not following that custom,' she added sweetly.

Prime ministerial audiences with The Queen are totally private. Callaghan spent some of these meetings strolling round Buckingham Palace gardens with The Queen, on warm summer evenings. On one such occasion, when the Prime Minister returned to the Palace, he was wearing a rose in his buttonhole. 'She picked it for me,' he said. He was proud and pleased, and he told everyone about it later.

All anecdotes about Edward Heath are true. He saw no need to make himself agreeable, and in my brief experiences of him he sank into a pool of silence at any purely social occasion, though he did have an occasional masterful ability to show contempt, as with his famous remark, 'I seldom attack the Labour Party. They do it so well themselves.'

I was seconded for two years to the Cabinet Office as part of the Assessment Staff of the Joint Intelligence Committee, which advised the Cabinet, and the prime minister in particular, on strategic issues relating to our overseas policies. In the view of its most senior diplomat of the time, Sir Percy Cradock, in his book *Know Your Enemy*, the Assessment Staff had a success rate which made it one of the most important British assets in our relationship with the United States on intelligence matters. This success contrasted dramatically with the ideologically inspired creation, the so-called 'Think Tank', which also operated from the Cabinet Office, and was, in my time there in the early seventies, headed up by Lord Victor Rothschild. It was meant to act as a sort of kitchen cabinet, an élite commando unit, set up to attack traditional Civil Service ways of decision-taking. Rothschild knew how important influence and persuasion were in that process, and so he went to the extent of getting his friend, the actress Dame Peggy Ashcroft, to coach his young team so that they could better persuade the most hardened Civil Servant or minister when arguing their case. It worked for a while, then Rothschild resigned, and the Civil Service swept back over the remains, until its final death in 1983 by the hand of Margaret Thatcher. She in turn brought in the Director General of the CBI, Sir John Hoskyns, as head of yet another new body, the Prime Ministerial Policy Unit. It is generally accepted that it, too, failed to achieve much, and Hoskyns' successor, the distinguished journalist Ferdinand Mount, would probably agree that, while his own personal influence was profound, the Unit itself made little lasting mark on the Civil Service system of the time.

Two of the most impressive politicians seen in close-up from the sidelines were hugely talented though they did not achieve the highest office. Idealists from the polar extremes of political life,

Tony Benn and Enoch Powell were frequently voted by their peers the two most effective speakers in the House of Commons. Whenever Powell spoke in the House, Margaret Thatcher would sit forward, listening to him with rapt attention, until she eventually disowned him, because here was a brilliant mind and a precise formulator of argument, even though, with his variously interpreted 'rivers of blood' speech, he was to banish himself into the political wilderness.

At the opposite end of the scale was Tony Benn, whom I helped look after when he came to New York as Minister of Energy. He too was a true conviction speaker, despite the fact that he had recently been accused by a fellow MP of having 'just completed the long road to the lunatic asylum of politics'. Unlike most ministers, he carried with him few if any files and papers, but he had a much consulted little notebook; if he did not know something, the notebook would reveal the name and telephone number of someone who did.

Tony Benn addressed the British American Chamber of Commerce one lunch-time in New York in the mid-seventies. He was greeted in almost total silence by the predominantly right-wing audience, because here was an extreme left-winger with the reputation of wanting to nationalise everything. But, by the end of his speech, in which he talked with great clarity about the huge promise of North Sea oil and argued the case for Britain's economic prosperity, he was given a standing ovation.

Tony Benn is one of those figures who has protected his shelf-life, despite the fact that he has not held ministerial office for almost a quarter of a century. Why? Because, with his calm, reasoned, if isolated left-wing views, he has become a great British institution, always available to the media, at any time and on almost any subject. He is a polished performer in every way. By his very manner, he gives the impression of getting to the heart of things; he sounds jovial when he talks, surrounded as he always seems to be by clouds of pipe smoke and mugs of milky tea.

The New York press can be fickle, but they covered Benn's New York visit extremely well, no doubt largely due to his diligent press secretary. He was none other than that most loyal, true-blue spindoctor from later years, Bernard Ingham, later to become Mrs Thatcher's most devoted aide. Now an irascibly constant feature on our television screens, he prompts a recall of Diderot's remark about Prince Orlov, 'He boils and boils, but seldom cooks.'

SIX

New York, New York

In a high wind, even turkeys fly.
American Indian saying

New York, New York, a tirade of impressions, a city of nations, a city of allegiances, streets filled with the shops and palaces of an affluent society, with the limos three feet longer than anywhere else in the world and the subways designed by Escher. In the early days, waves of immigrants stuck together to defend themselves. Outsiders were out. When posted there by the Foreign Office in the mid-seventies, we eventually found a splendid thirtieth-floor apartment on Upper East Side, but, before we could rent it, we had to be interviewed by the Residents' Scrutiny Committee to ensure we were suitable. There was one lone African American tenant in the building to ensure impartiality. He was called O.J. Simpson. We also passed.

Suitability was everything. If you went into the foyer of one of the old, old blocks in that part of Manhattan, you could still see, on a framed notice by the doorway, that apartments there might be available to rent. These notices were often painted in elaborate gilt lettering, the words varnished over many times. Maybe you can still see, at the foot of the board, where a small rectangle has been carefully painted over: I did so, on more than one occasion. The obliterated word, painted in small letters, once read 'RESTRICTED', meaning no Jews. Yet New York is very much a Jewish city, where laughter goes along with anxiety, like that famous New York Jewish telegram, 'Start worrying. Details follow.'

It is also an Irish city, and for a long time the Irish were also seen as being unsuitable. Michael Shea is my name and I had a third-generation Irish American grandfather, whose own father was a mercenary who was serving with the Maryland Regiment when he was killed at Gettysburg. That bit of my background forces the memory of an Irish pub somewhere on Third Avenue, and the old sign that hung there, venerated for all the wrong reasons. It had never originally hung in that locale, for it had the badly painted letters 'NINA' on it – 'No Irish Need Apply'. They displayed such warnings outside many a shop and employment agency in New York City, until well into living memory.

Fast-forwarding to an evening in the mid-seventies, I was already prepared for ethnic tensions when I got off the ferry and, after losing my way for a bit, eventually entered that upper room of the church hall on Staten Island. Inside it was hot and crowded. From the start it was not a sympathetic audience. I had found my way there to take part in a lively, no, a very angry debate about Northern Ireland. As a diplomat, currently a Director in British Information Services – the propaganda arm of the British government in New York – it was one of my less easy duties, and the timing was terrible. Noraid was in its prime, angry American Senators were against us, British policies had few friends, a large section of New York's St Patrick's Day Parade deviated from Fifth Avenue and marched across to stop outside the British Government Offices on Third Avenue to demonstrate, while Bobby Sands was on a hunger strike and on the point of death.

I made my speech, which went down badly. I was heckled more than I had ever been, and my attempts to lighten the tone failed miserably. My main opponent was a diminutive Roman Catholic priest who stood at the back of the room, shouting his interruptions at my every argument. After the questions, and before the meeting closed, he again yelled, 'Change yer name or change yer allegiance, Mr Michael Shea!'

Later, as I was leaving, he came up to me, shook my hand warmly and told me I had done well in the circumstances. Then he walked me down to the ferry, where we stopped for a glass of Irish whiskey to set me on my way.

In recent years, I have seldom had to stand on such controversial political hustings, facing an antagonistic audience or much heckling from the floor. All the old asides – 'Sorry, I can't hear you', 'Am I interrupting you?', 'Can you speak up so that we all can hear?', 'You've obviously been drinking in self-defence!' or, more aggressively, if most of the audience is with you, 'I see not only the walls are plastered!' – have been put to bed with other under-graduate debating gimmicks.

We all have to listen to speeches from time to time, and while the content may be sound, if the delivery fails, the message will be lost. Many years spent teaching public speaking and communications skills proves the simple fact: all too few of those who climb on to the public stage communicate with any real clarity or conviction. Listen to the neanderthal grunts of the average football or tennis star, let alone the incoherence of many captains of industry or back-bench MPs, to prove that on a daily basis.

The greatest speeches have been where the beginning and the end came close together. The Gettysburg Address took a mere two minutes to deliver, and is only 274 words long, with Abraham Lincoln admitting that he always worked on the assumption that his audience had an average age of eight. Judging by much contemporary rhetoric, things have not advanced much since then, particularly in the United States, where to quote that magnificent former British Ambassador to Washington, Sir Nico Henderson, 'The Americans devour bad speeches the way goats do waste paper.' Incidentally, he is one public figure whose rhetoric disarms his often highly eccentric appearance. His diaries, published despite much disapproval from former colleagues, demonstrated that a modern ambassador is no mere postman or hotelier, but can wield great influence, as Henderson did in Washington on Britain's behalf during the Falklands War. I remember last talking to him at a Buckingham Palace reception some time ago, as he stood, white tie and waistcoat all askew, with medals and decorations pinned all over the place on his tailcoat like a Christmas tree, while the grandest of all his orders hung by a broad ribbon, not neatly to one side as it should, but like an errant sporran there to protect his dynasty.

In New York, certain people kept reappearing in my life in the most unexpected of ways. I had a splendid office on Third Avenue, to which I returned one day from a bibulous lunch at the Dutch Treat Club. They were a group of famously stimulating Manhattan saints and sinners, who followed the odd New York habit of serving huge dry martinis before lunch, accompanied only by coffee, who listened to the most marvellous speeches from their strikingly eclectic fellow members. In consequence, I was looking forward to a post-prandial snooze, but it was not to be.

Arriving back at my office, I was greeted by my secretary, Mary, who had an unusually worried expression on her face. 'Said he was an MP. He's taken over your office, and is using both your phones . . . at the same time,' she said, disapprovingly.

Robert Maxwell had indeed taken over my office. 'Hope you don't mind,' he said generously as I walked in, not even bothering to stand up from behind my desk. He had in tow a sharp-looking male assistant and a too-pretty secretary, and even they were looking a fraction ill at ease. Mary had been correct when she reported that he had said he was an MP, with *was* the operative word. He had ceased being the MP for Buckingham in 1970.

'Just fixing up a meeting with the President. Hoping to print his collected speeches,' said Maxwell.

Who was I to argue with a man speaking to the White House from my office, for I knew that Mr Maxwell had produced the collected speeches of lots of world leaders, not least those of my old friend Ceauşescu. After an hour or so he left, and to this day I wonder if it was indeed the President of the United States he was trying to arrange this deal with, or was he being economical with the truth in a way that he became famous for, and it was some other president from some far less democratic nation? By coincidence, my boss, Peter Jay, at the time the British Ambassador in Washington, later joined Maxwell's staff as his gopher. With remarks like 'Go get my car, Peter', I saw Maxwell set out to humiliate that able man, particularly when important company was present. It was a further measure of a bully's style.

After the exigencies of Romania, New York was in one sense a promised land. On the bad news front, while we had always been safe in Bucharest's streets, even late at night, it was not so in pre-Giuliani New York. A mere two days after arriving I was mugged, one man banging hard into my left shoulder and making my jacket swing open, thereby giving easy access to my wallet pocket to his accomplice. On the positive side, our first visit to a supermarket in three years left us bewildered by choice. We suddenly had a dozen varieties of margarine to choose from, when, back in Romania, there were none, and it took us some time to get used to conspicuous consumption once more.

We discovered many other things about New York we had not expected, like the cockroaches that were endemic, even on the thirtieth floor of our upper-class building, and of a size that rivalled the largest ones we had found in Romania. Then there was that compellingly nanny-ish ad on television every evening, when a gloom-filled, lugubrious voice came on saying: 'It's 10 p.m. Do you know where your children are?'

More crucial to our carefully monitored children was their first discovery of a McDonalds, which the family had never seen before that first New York evening in 1976. The trouble was, it was sited next door to a porn movie house on Second Avenue, and the explicit pictures outside were something of a distraction to our young children. My own very personal problem was with our apartment: I do not have a head for heights, and the windows on the thirtieth floor stretched from ceiling to floor, even in the bathrooms. I used to crawl around in the middle of the rooms, and when I first arrived took to wearing dark glasses, never nearing the balcony to look at the views. But that phobia proved to be all in the mind; by the end of our years there, I was happily leaning far out of the windows to clean them.

The other unexpected thing I discovered, as everyone new to NYC does, were the extremes of weather, and the fact that temperatures can change rapidly in the course of a few hours. The views from our apartment were sensational in all directions, but never more so than on that winter's day in the mid-seventies, when there was a total white-out, and metres of snow fell. The streets were deserted, with gentle hills showing where the buses and cars lay silent underneath, and only one solitary figure, my Norwegian wife, on skis, free from all worries of being mugged, *langlauf*-ing the whole length of Second Avenue.

I had little to do with the United Nations while I was posted to New York, but some years earlier, I had, for a week or so, been a junior member of the British Delegation to the General Assembly, bag-carrying for Alec Douglas-Home. Every time I went into that building, I wondered at the skills of the original interior design engineers, for the illuminations were so subtle, and the carpets and walls so carefully shaded that almost all the diplomats parading the corridors, or conspiring in the ante-rooms, ended up looking exactly the same colour. Clever that, as was the common drink of the day, the Bloody Mary, which, at that time of heightened East–West tensions, remained basically Russian and yet intrinsically American.

These were great times, with great New York characters, and Walter Cronkite among them. He was the man of whom it was said that no one believed the evening news until they had heard him tell it. This was and is a man with a 100 per cent credibility rating. He said of himself, 'I give the people the news; I don't tell them how I think,' and again 'I am a news presenter, a news broadcaster, and anchorman; a managing editor, not a commentator or analyst.' As for his opinion of the British media, he gave a despairing shrug and refused to be drawn further when I asked, beyond saying that a nation gets the media it deserves. Surely he was wrong there.

The mix of fact and opinion, the scourge of the modern media, along with the distracting gestures and hand-waving that is currently fashionable on British television, was absent in Cronkite. But that did not mean he lacked an acute analytical mind, and used it behind the scenes. Outwardly, he came with no spin. When he came to dinner one night, he and our other guests stayed encouragingly late; then, as the Cronkites were leaving, his wife revealed that it was now his sixtieth birthday. So we opened the champagne and started all over again. Many years later we met up again in London and had tea together with his wife Patsy. When I told him we were off to a reception at the American Ambassador's residence, in Regent's Park, he remembered that he too had been invited, so we shared a car. The ambassador of the day was far from being up to the usual standard. When we came into the reception room to shake hands, our host greeted me warmly, since we had been in contact over a forthcoming presidential visit. I then ushered forward Walter Cronkite, one of the best-known faces in all the United States, with the words, 'Your next guest needs no introduction . . .'.

He did. The ambassador stared blankly at him, unrecognising, because he did not expect him, and, without a word, turned to his next guest. It took an embarrassed Embassy social secretary ages to get her ambassador to come up and say how sorry he was.

In New York I dealt with serious journalists and serious journalism, though tabloids are tabloids the world over. I have, from my time there, the following quote, typed on a piece of yellowing paper given me by David Frost:

In America, journalism has carried its authority to the grossest and most brutal extreme. As a natural consequence, it has begun to create a spirit of revolt. People are amused by it or disgusted by it, according to their temperaments. But it is no longer the real force it was. It is not seriously treated. In England, journalism, except in a few well-known instances, not having been carried to such excesses of brutality, is still a great factor, a really remarkable power. The tyranny that it proposes to exercise over people's private lives seems to me to be quite extraordinary. The fact is that the public have an insatiable curiosity to know everything, except what is worth knowing.

Such a comparison between the media on both sides of the Atlantic may seem a little dated. The writer, more famously, wrote, 'In the old days men had the rack. Now they have the press.' Oscar Wilde wrote the longer quote, in 1890, and enough of it remains true to this day. Having dealt with the media for substantial periods on both sides of the Atlantic, I knew that Britain and America had always fed off each other's style of journalism. It was easy to forget that a Scot, James Gordon Bennett, who died in 1872, was the man who first introduced scandalous yellow journalism to the New World, and that the American Ralph David Blumenfeld, who came to London as a self-defined 'royal watcher', to cover Queen Victoria's Jubilee, not only stayed on, but in 1904 became Editor in Chief of the *Daily Express*, a post he was to hold for a record-breaking twenty-eight years. Sadly, it has always been at the muck-raking end of the market, where myth and reality blend into one, that such cross-fertilisation of talent has thrived.

At the other end of the scale, Mrs Thatcher, now leader of the Opposition, came into my life once more while I was in New York, when I escorted her to lunch with the distinguished Editorial Board of the *Wall Street Journal*. With great clarity, she gave them her view of world economic problems for most of the meal, but, just once, she seemed to flip and forget to whom she was talking. Having held these hardest of hard men of the press riveted, she suddenly began explaining, in the simplest of language, her daily shopping habits, and how she knew the price of milk and instant coffee, as if she was addressing a group of elderly and highly sceptical constituents, and trying to show them that she still had the common touch. Some of these hard-nosed journalists and editors turned to each other, exchanging meaningful glances while looking at their watches, but, just in time, the lady reverted to type, and the lunch was saved.

If the Dutch Treat Club was one New York joy, the Algonquin Hotel was another. Of course its glory days had long gone, but the ghosts of Robert Benchley and Dorothy Parker still lingered, and the current limelighters of the *New Yorker* came there to long-lunch, and talk of literature and the arts, embroidered with their own wit and repartee. That other hotel, the Carlyle, was another watering hole, though it was never as strange as, long after I had left the Palace and was in New York to promote Scotland, that occasion late one night when I found myself in the peculiar position of having been asked to introduce Sarah, the Duchess of York as she still was, who was staying in the hotel, to Eartha Kitt, who was standing by the piano, entertaining the late night guests with her songs. I have never seen such long eyelashes, such a tight dark face, and such cold determination. Eartha Kitt had absolutely no intention of being upstaged by any visiting flame-haired duchess. As introductions go it scored zero out of ten. The singer's face scarcely flickered, she totally ignored the outstretched hand, then turned and swept from the room.

New York is a city of unity and rivalry, of pride and prejudice, like so many others. From postwar Berlin on to Biafra in Nigeria, from Belfast, where I received a brief indoctrination in the problems there before they were exported to New York, then Bucharest, where deep-lasting bitterness between Romania and Hungary still exists over their centuries-old territorial claims on Transylvania, ethnic distrust and hatreds still fester under the film of civilisation. An archbishop once told me of talking to a West Indian child in North Belfast, and asking him if he were Catholic or Protestant. 'Hell, no, Sir,' came the clear reply. 'Neither. I have a hard enough time being black.'

Such sectarian rivalries, promoted by religious extremism, along with all its postwar dirt and squalor, was why I had detested the Glasgow of my childhood, though with age and experience I have come to respect the city a little more. It is true: a Glasgow funeral has more life to it than a wedding in my home town of Edinburgh, and admittedly my city's prejudices are merely better hidden, as, centuries ago, David Hume, Edinburgh's most celebrated philosopher, found when he could not get his work published there, and had to go to Bristol to find a printer. Glasgow's ethnic evils bubble to the surface, and not just of the Rangers–Celtic supporters variety; they are endemic in much of its society. I have a Jewish Glaswegian friend, who at school was always challenged: 'But are you a Protestant Jew or a Catholic Jew?'; and anyone responding to the apparently innocent question 'Which school did you go to?' is immediately categorised.

My first ever taste of prejudice was near Dunoon, the 'Glasgow-on-holiday' town, sometime in the late forties. I was on a brief stay with my parents, one of the first possible retreats after the war. In a small hotel directly facing the rocky beach, on that very first evening, I was comfortably installed with a book when I heard raised voices by the reception desk. Although rooms were available, the hotelier had that afternoon refused accommodation to a German-Jewish refugee family. My father checked us out immediately in protest and we moved to another hotel, followed, at his urging, by a few other guests, discomforted by his 'that's what we've just fought Hitler for'.

My long retired, German-Jewish neighbour tells me that Jews never stayed in hotels in pre-war Nazi Germany. He, in his childhood, had to move schools, to quote his headmaster, so that his 'specific needs' might be met. Shades again of that notice 'Restricted' in New York City. But prejudice is alive and well in modern London too. A Jewish parent present at a famous central London Church of England school's open day was told by the headmistress in front of a significant audience that their child 'surely would be happier with its own kind'. We could not believe our ears. Because our daughters were not baptised, they too were at first refused entry, until the headmistress heard that I was to be working at Buckingham Palace; so that was all right then, and we were to be welcomed. Needless to say, we went elsewhere.

In 1995 I wrote an article in the London *Evening Standard*, defending Malcolm Rifkind (not that he needed defending), who had become Foreign Secretary in the middle of that year. The *Spectator*, in a most curious article, questioned his suitability for the job in a way that said more about the writer of the article than its subject. It dwelt, for example, on Rifkind's East European Jewish family origins, as if that mattered, and then went on to complain that he had 'the vanity of speaking' at great length and without notes. As letter-writers to the magazine had expressed their outrage, I merely commented that if any of his fellow front-bench spokesmen, from either party, had been able to marshal their words with half the drama and sense of purpose as Rifkind, even with notes, democracy would be much better served.

One last glimpse is of what, I hope, was a light-hearted show of prejudice. Members of the Foreign Office who were waiting for a new posting were often utilised, for a few days and weeks, to 'weed' or thin out old files – superfluous drafts or duplicates of letters and so on, to make the papers more manageable and less bulky in storage. I came across one late wartime Foreign Office memorandum containing a diplomatic report of Moscow's secret overtures to the Vatican. Across it, in the distinctive red ink of a prime minister, Winston Churchill had written, 'If the communists and the Catholics ever get together, we'll be destroyed. W.S.C.'

Much later an official had written, 'This memo must be destroyed'. Thankfully, successive generations ignored that command.

The turning points of life move one to other challenges, and change one life into another. I had just helped HMG finish one key task, getting Concorde its landing rights in New York. There had been a huge campaign against the plane: quite apart from the noise level, it was going to give everyone cancer and so on. Interestingly, no mention was made of the real reason for the opposition, which was that the British and French had, for once, beaten the Americans at bringing commercial supersonic flight to the world's travellers. The campaign had gone on for years, and consumed huge amounts of time, effort and money on both sides. We won, and the day that Concorde landed at JFK my job was to help the British press find the remaining protesters. Eventually we found a dozen of them, miserable-looking, sheltering from the rain under a flyover in Queens.

Then, one lunch-time some days later, overnight bag packed, I was about to leave my office to fly to Chicago to give another speech on Northern Ireland. The telephone on my desk rang. I hesitated, wondering whether to answer it or not. I just had time and picked up the receiver. It was my ambassador in Washington, telling me that he was pulling me off what I was doing, and that I was ordered to help organise the forthcoming visit by The Queen on the occasion of the American Bicentennial Year. I tried to argue. I knew nothing about the royal family, I said. I failed. I had genuinely never really thought about the monarchy, except when I received my national service and diplomatic commissions with The Queen's sign manual at the top right of the document. That call changed my life and career. Later, the ambassador told me that if he had failed to reach me, he would simply have chosen one of the other First Secretaries from the Embassy.

The visit itself was a huge success. I first saw The Queen at a garden party reception, in the grounds of the British Embassy in Washington. My duties were with the media, and I tried to control the camera teams as they followed her around the lawns. It was getting dark, and a dozen high-powered television lights were on her – so how she could possibly see beyond them I did not know. Then, suddenly, total darkness, and I was aware that the TV cameramen and the stills photographers were racing back up the lawn to where the guests had come in. Protocol had stated that they all should be there well before The Queen began her walkabout. The Vice-President was there already. Since the Embassy is British territory, the President himself would arrive after The Queen, so this must be him. But no: it was Elizabeth Taylor, making her grand entrance, which left The Queen, with a very angry ambassador to guide her, stumbling along in the darkness. She, I noticed, was merely amused at seeing, for once, someone else as the centre of media attention. That little scene repeated itself much later, when she gave a party for Prince Andrew at Buckingham Palace. The guests were mainly young, and I saw her standing, after dinner, all alone, as she watched the youthful revellers crowd ten deep around Elton John. Such is fame.

New York, New York. While we lived there, I remember a well-known legal case being pursued between a city cleric and the Internal Revenue Service, which had allowed his tax claim to a subscription to *Playboy* but not to the *Wall Street Journal*, because the latter 'lacked social relevance'. And how can we forget the farewell dinner when we left New York, which was given for us in the restaurant at the very top of the Trade Towers?

SEVEN

Waiting for the President

Greatness in the Presidential chair is largely an illusion of the people.

Time Magazine

There is an inbuilt need, particularly for weak leaders – think of all those South American coups – to parade, with their senior generals flanked around them, as a show of unity for the cameras and the people beyond. George W. Bush does it to add weight to his naïve, 'what, me?' image, with the strength of Powell and Condoleezza Rice as his supporters. Not so with Ronald Reagan. His colleagues flitted in and out, but usually well beyond the spotlights. Reagan was enough on his own, but the behind-the-scenes programming was exactly the same.

It was 1982, and we were waiting, in excellent company, for the President of the United States of America. The Queen and the Duke of Edinburgh had accepted an invitation from President and Mrs Reagan to pay a State Visit, not to Washington this time, but to his home state of California, and it had been a splendid few days. The Queen, having already visited Mexico, travelled on board *Britannia*, which in itself was a huge crowd-puller, all the way up the coast, from San Diego to Seattle. But the high point of the visit was Santa Barbara, where the President wished to host The Queen at his private ranch, high in the hills above that pretty, and very-civilised-for-California, town.

There were acts of God aplenty that week. We had a mini-tornado. We had an earthquake. We had torrential rain. We had floods. The night before the visit to Santa Barbara, President and Mrs Reagan had stayed the night on board the royal yacht, which was all very relaxed, and we even had a sing-song after dinner with Mrs Reagan and Mike Deaver, the President's Deputy Chief of Staff, at the piano. The next morning it was very different. The skies had opened again and the quayside was flooded to a depth of about a metre, thereby preventing the low-slung presidential limousine fleet from getting to the bottom of *Britannia*'s gangway. Duckboards and pontoons were played around with to little advantage. So we stood around waiting, an informal group of us, in the foyer outside the yacht's state drawing-room, until a US Navy bus could be found that would ride high enough on its axles to ferry us to the fleet of waiting VIP cars.

The small group stood waiting: The Queen, the Duke of Edinburgh, two private secretaries, a policeman, myself. On the other side, President and Mrs Reagan, two secret servicemen, and a bunch of White House staffers who had waded across to the yacht, principally Michael Deaver. The Queen watched and waited for a period of fifteen to twenty minutes while various aides came up to the President and said things like, 'Your thinking on Nicaragua this morning, Mr President, is as follows . . .', or, 'If you're asked about Reserve Bank interest rates, Mr President, you should say the following . . .', or, 'Mr President, your policy on the Middle East, following recent developments, goes like this . . .'. Finally, Mike Deaver came up with a copy of a speech which the President was to deliver later that morning, and said something like, 'Mr President, I'm sorry you haven't seen the text of your speech until now, but we've broken it up in the normal way, with pronunciation guides to the various difficult names. You may want to read it through, but I am sure you will do OK, if you don't have time. Sorry you haven't seen it before.'

We also heard Reagan's other key adviser, Alexander Haig, saying things like, 'You should remember, Mr President, that your position on the SALT talks is . . .'. They spoke openly in these briefing sessions, reminding the President what he might have forgotten, or telling him things he quite obviously did not know in the first place. But that is politics, no matter where. Later, Peggy Noonan, Reagan's speech-writer, was to admit, famously, that 'the battle for the mind of Ronald Reagan was like trench warfare in World War One. Never have so many battled so hard over such barren terrain.'

Standing waiting on the deck of *Britannia*, The Queen, having been fascinated by this briefing process, turned with a faint smile to her entourage, who would never have dared land a speech on her at the last moment, and, in a louder than stage whisper, said, 'And who do they call a Constitutional Monarch?'

There was another hiccup before we descended the gangway to get on to the US Navy bus. Nancy Reagan pointed to her husband, who was wrapped up in a belted, fawn trench coat, and said, 'Have you got it on, Ronnie?'

'No, Nancy.' He looked shifty.

We British spectators were polite onlookers, bemused and baffled.

Mrs Reagan folded her hands. 'I'm not going anywhere 'til you go put it on.'

We watched, curiosity showing on all our faces.

'Oh gee, Nancy, it's so hot.'

'Don't care.'

'OK, I'll do it.' The President of the United States shrugged, took off his trench coat, and went back down to his cabin to re-emerge, struggling his way into a heavy bullet-proof vest. He was then helped by one of his aides into the trench coat again. One could only sympathise with both husband and wife. He looked stiff, hot, and very uncomfortable. On the other hand, Nancy Reagan had lived through the attempted assassination in March 1981, when he took those bullets through his chest as he was leaving a Washington hotel, then bravely joked with the team of surgeons, as he was being wheeled into the operating theatre, 'I hope you're all Republicans.'

Another time, another visit to the States, but on this occasion, strictly private. The Queen had been invited to visit the manicured equestrian farms of Kentucky, followed by a very different private stay in the wilds around Little Big Horn in Wyoming. But first, arrangements had to be made for that privacy to happen. We had to tell the media that she was coming, but that there would only be one or two press calls, and that the rest was strictly private.

I went to the White House in advance, to see my opposite number, the eponymously named Larry Speakes, the President's Press Secretary. I showed him my draft press release that read 'Queen to visit studs in Kentucky'.

Larry took my arm and gently pulled me into a corner. 'Mike,' he said quietly, 'I have, just to begin with, and I don't quite know how to say this, a bit of a problem with the word "Queen".'

We redrafted, and later put out a press release with the headline 'Her Majesty Queen Elizabeth II to visit Stallion Stations in Kentucky.'

Incidentally, Larry Speakes was the spokesman who, after the Reykjavik Summit between Presidents Reagan and Gorbachev, announced to the press that Reagan had said something on the lines of 'Mr First Secretary, we may not have agreed on many things here in Iceland, but the world breathes easier because we are meeting here today.'

It was a good quote that hit the headlines all round the world. Later, however, Larry committed the ultimate sin, by admitting in his memoirs that he himself had made up the quote, without reference to either the President or his senior advisers. He was immediately dismissed from his new job in Wall Street, and was widely excoriated, not for telling the truth, but for pulling aside the veil from the practice of spindoctoring.

When things go wrong in life, it is usually to do with such ill-judged communication. Who have been the great communicators in each of our lives? Was it some schoolteacher, or university professor, or was it a gifted political or business leader who moved us when they spoke? Whom do we listen to and why do we reach for the off button when others come into sight? That ex-film star,

President Reagan, the Teflon man, was always known in the States as the great communicator, just as the George Bushes, father and son, are known for their ability, despite all the programming they are given, to go to war with the English language. Meeting George Bush the First, when he was still Vice-President, I shared a limousine with him and his wife on The Queen's visit to California, and I still have the trousers with the slight tear in the leg from when, standing beside the door of the vice-presidential limousine, waiting for President Reagan to arrive in his helicopter, Mr Bush pushed me forcefully down behind the car on to some gravel, to avoid my being caught in the vast whirlwind of dust and debris as the helicopter landed.

Much later, he frankly admitted in a speech in London that if he had communicated better (the world waited, for example, for a ringing speech of triumph when the Berlin Wall came down, but got only badly-rehearsed platitudes), and had known how to string sentences together with some resonance, he believed he would have won a second term in office. It is a defect that his son, with notorious remarks such as 'I'm worried that more and more of our imports come from overseas,' has fully inherited. When the father ran against Dukakis in 1988, the passion vacuum was horrifying, but he won because, even though he talked like a stumbling grandmother, Dukakis, in his built-up shoes, was even duller and more wooden in comparison. A polled 75 per cent of the American electorate at the time said that they went for Bush on the basis of gut instinct, and his 'looks' as a candidate, and not on the policies that either man stood for, despite Bush, as the saying had it, being like Gerald Ford without the articulacy. History repeats itself: we remember Dubya versus Gore.

President Ford was the man of whom it was said he could not walk and chew gum at the same time: a harsh judgement, but his repeated verbal stumbles also marked his career more than his successes. It was reported that he said on one occasion, 'I say that if Lincoln were living today, he would turn over in his grave,' and, even more embarrassingly, he once toasted Anwar Sadat as 'the

President of Israel!', a mistake that President Reagan came close to emulating some time later.

On one visit to Washington, introduced to ex-President Ford by the Duke of Edinburgh, I later talked to him when I spotted him standing, totally alone, in the corner of a grand reception for The Queen, given by his successor, Ronald Reagan. He was most approachable, with a good knowledge of the political situation in Britain, and we chatted for some time, no one coming forward to interrupt a junior British official talking to an ex-President. When, eventually, I moved on, I turned briefly and saw him alone once more.

This stimulates memories of a lengthy conversation in New York with Pierre Salinger, President Kennedy's Press Secretary, about various presidents' communication skills. He talked about the audience research they did on the famous Kennedy–Nixon debates on television and radio in the sixties. When polled, the television audience overwhelmingly went for the handsome, clean-cut Kennedy, as opposed to the grim, five-o'clock-shadowed Richard Nixon, the man of whom it was to be said 'you never believe a thing until Nixon has denied it twice', and who, according to David Frost, actually said, 'When the President does it, that means it's not illegal'.

On the other hand, Salinger explained how the radio audience of the day, denied access to the visual advantages and drawbacks of the two candidates, came out overwhelmingly in favour of Nixon, with his gravelly, authoritative voice, against the hesitant words of the still immature John Fitzgerald Kennedy.

It is all to do with the 'primacy effect', the first few seconds of seeing anyone for the first time, when, no matter how skilled or broad-minded we may think we are, we make instantaneous judgements about those we meet socially, in a business environment, or see on our television screens. Some sixth sense or gut instinct tells us which person to trust, to listen to, or vote for. Time is usually too short, from the myriad choices we have to make all the time, to hesitate too long in our judgements. No matter how complex the people we meet may be, unless we get to know them over time, we pigeon hole them with some single, dismissive adjective, pinned firmly against their names. As the advertisement has it, they don't have a second chance to make a first impression.

As a former head-hunter, I found that no matter how much background information we dug up on individuals on the short list of candidates for a top job, no matter how excellently polished and groomed their CVs were, and even when their candidature came with the most glowing testimonials (and if you want rid of someone from your empire, you send them on their way with excellently window-dressed references) the one that looked the part and communicated best, rather than the best-qualified, won the day. Unfair but true, again and again and again. How many candidates for a job or promotion, and how many strategies have bitten the dust in between the candidate coming in the door of the interview room and sitting down at the green baize table? The central casting scenario always comes into play, for why else do we have interviews?

We push people vigorously into their slots, and do not let them out again without their doing something fairly dramatic to cause us to change our judgements. Our retained images of Kinnock, Major, Hague, Ashdown or Kennedy, let alone Thatcher and Blair, deserve more description, but, as they slip into the memory pile, they become like Churchill that 'great war leader', or Diana 'the people's Princess', and what else besides?

Distractions of dress, body language, accent, and the paralanguage that is built up out of the cadences, the flow, the resonance and authority of a person's voice, explain why some people in life are listened to, and why we turn away when others appear before us, either in real life or on the television screens. We have seen well-turned-out people, with looks, clothes and hair, all done to perfection, who, the moment they open their mouths, become tragically flawed. People are attracted by the way others speak. If someone is powerful or melodious in their diction, they will appeal. If an untrained screech or dreadful vowel sounds emerge, they are lost. Pulling yourself up by your vocal chords is a great way to a better career – although, having trained many key people in public speaking skills over the years, I have never required any of them to get rid of their inherited accents, unless that, or poor articulation, got in the way of others understanding them.

The language of leadership has a huge effect on image. We learn to speak between the ages of two and five, but few of us have any subsequent training in how to speak properly to an audience, a strange phenomenon in a world where only a few public people get listened to, whatever they say, while the many are a total switch-off as soon as they open their mouths. In the mid-1960s, Harold Wilson was able to mock the then Prime Minister, Sir Alec Douglas-Home, by revealing that Eldon Griffiths and Nigel Lawson wrote his speeches for him. We now know that Wilson, a man who made a speciality out of small misjudgements, had a huge amount of help in his turn, just as Douglas Hurd cut his teeth writing the words for Edward Heath, and Ronald Miller, the playwright, put key phrases into Margaret Thatcher's mouth, such as 'the Lady's not for turning'. Even George Washington had Alexander Hamilton to help him write his greatest lines. John Major spoke by rote, in prosy English, sounding like that seer from the first days of the National Lottery, Mystic Meg, while his successors, William Hague and Iain Duncan Smith, sterling performers at Prime Minister's Questions, failed to carry the necessary conviction away from the House of Commons. Is it really that alpha-male factor, linked to dominant evolutionary success, that sinks politicians in the end?

Leadership is not just about communication, but also about posture and looks. Shaw said that you could always tell an Englishman by the fact that he could say 'really!' in eleven different ways. 'You're late!' said to a spouse, can mean many things too, from good-humoured resignation to blind fury. A clenched fist, a smile or a scowl, can speak a thousand words, as can a woman with one too many buttons undone on her blouse, though my favourite example of blunt communication by what you wear, was the once-sighted sign on the back of a passing motorcyclist's black leather jacket which stated, 'If you can read this, the wife's fallen off.'

Mrs Thatcher, speaking to an American audience in the late eighties, had this encouragement: 'Let our children grow tall, and some taller than others if they have it in them to do so.' *The Economist*, with its tongue not too firmly in its cheek, took up her remark and argued that, in the industrial Britain of the day, height added to perceived competence, and that tall leaders such as Lord Hanson at six feet five inches, and his partner, Sir Gordon White, at six feet six inches, would always win out over the likes of Sir Michael Edwardes, the then Chairman of Dunlop, who came in at a mere five foot four. Of course Hitler and Napoleon were small men, and Madonna and Dustin Hoffman are each only five foot four high, so there are other things to be factored into any such equation.

As an aside, Helen Young, the weather-woman at the BBC, admitted that when she was giving the forecast she was so small that she had to stand on a box, otherwise 'I would never have reached the Hebrides'; but it is the perception of being in charge of what is going on that matters to the outside world.

The first royal blood I saw was in America, on the streets of Chicago. It was 1976, and Prince Charles was on a grand tour of the States, including Hollywood, if only to be photographed with the glamorous stars of *Charlie's Angels*, of course. Well before my going to Buckingham Palace, I had been seconded to help with the press covering the tour, with first stop that great northern city. The entire centre was closed to traffic, and the Prince did a long walkabout. Crowds, mainly of women clutching bunches of flowers, screamed 'Charlie, Charlie'. Almost never, except once when I saw Elvis from afar, have I seen so many hysterical women. Prince Charles, young and unmarried, walked along shaking hands, thousands upon thousands of them. I thought nothing of it until, afterwards, in his hotel suite, he showed us his already huge hands, swollen to twice their normal size, and covered in dozens of bloody cuts from the diamond rings of his fervent admirers who had grasped him so tightly. 'It's why The Queen wears gloves,' he said simply.

During that visit the Prince went to lunch at Walter Annenberg's opulent mansion. Mr Annenberg had been Ambassador to London and the invitation had been on the table for a long time. His house stood amid a beautifully kept private golf course, behind a thick band of tall trees that created their own mini-climate for the super-rich in that desert setting. We were shown his treasured Hall of Memories, stacked floor to ceiling with photographs, framed testimonials and plaques, while on the other walls of the house hung original French Impressionist paintings.

At the lunch table I was seated beside a very silent Frank Sinatra. He seemed to be in a world of his own, picking at the food on his plate without ever putting anything into his mouth. Perhaps he was on sedatives, for the scars of a recent facelift ran bright scarlet around the back of his ears and behind his neck. Don't mention the war: don't look at the scars. It was an impossible task.

Shortly after their marriage, the Prince and Princess of Wales visited the United States together. Much of it was a blur because of the insatiable demands of a huge media party, but I remember asking my opposite number at the White House, Larry Speakes, how the numbers of press and camera teams, standing high on specially built scaffolding on the White House lawn, compared with the numbers for the Pope, who had been there the previous week. 'About double,' he said.

At dinner that night, President Reagan proposed a toast to the happy couple, though what he actually said as he raised his glass was 'to Prince Charles and Princess Andrew'. It was a memorable night in many other ways. Sitting beside Peter Ustinov, with the great social hostess Drue Heinz on my other side, the former kept us regaled with stories of his recent trip to a Japanese bathhouse, and how he had had to negotiate his naked bulk down on to a tiny wooden three-legged stool. He had no worries about his nakedness until a petite lady assistant came up to him and asked, in perfect English, 'Would you like a cup of tea?' which had made him rush in embarrassment for his towel. That was the night when John Travolta danced with the Princess. The rest of us, like watchers at the first dance of a wedding, stood and gaped until the Prince of Wales at last wheeled Nancy Reagan on to the floor.

Peter Ustinov commented on the humour that added sanity to the insanity of political posturing on both sides of the Atlantic. As professionals on the sidelines, watching events from the wings, we needed to laugh a lot to keep going, and it was usually of the kindly variety. Long live cartoonists, parliamentary sketch-writers, and those who work for *Private Eye*, for otherwise the petty vanities of public life would inflate themselves beyond control. In Communist Romania, a banned underworld of political humour kept the spirit of freedom more alive than any public demonstration would ever have been able to do. Mockery is the supreme weapon against the self-obsessed.

American humour, in particular, hit me hard on my first student trip to Washington, DC, in 1962. Of the nation's capital it was said that it was the only place on earth where sound travelled faster than light, and JFK had allegedly defined it as a city of Southern efficiency and Northern charm. I had never seen a hot-air hand-drier in a men's washroom before, and this one had a slogan above it that read, 'Press here for a message from your Senator.' On one of my more recent trips to the capital, at the height of the Bush/Gore presidential campaign, I delighted in a bumper sticker reading, 'Thank God only one of them can win,' together with the *Washington Post* headline: 'George W. Bush, a man unknown throughout America, is now unknown throughout the world.'

At another Washington dinner, Christopher Soames, Churchill's son-in-law, told the story about the Prime Minister and the US Secretary of State, John Foster Dulles (of the mischievous 'Dull, duller, Dulles' fame), joking with each other. Dulles pats Churchill's substantial stomach and asks, 'Expecting, Winston? Boy or girl? What you goin' to call it?'

Churchill answers quietly, 'If it's a boy, it'll be George. If it's a girl, Elizabeth. But if, as I suspect, it's just wind, I'll call it John Foster Dulles.' Since being told that version I have heard it related to other politicians on both sides of the Atlantic, including

F.E. Smith talking to a Lord Chief Justice, and President Taft joking with a US Senator.

Later, at an Embassy dinner in London, the avuncular US Ambassador to the Court of St James was caught out smoking a large Havana cigar. How could he defend this when there was a strict American embargo on all Cuban exports?

'Easy . . . just burning the enemy's crops,' he explained, with a defiant puff.

Which leads easily on to the story, told by the same Ambassador, about the late Vice-President, Spiro Agnew, who was flying out of Washington on a scheduled flight and found himself sitting in first class beside an elegant young lady, who was, in those pre-tobacco-and-health days, also smoking a large Havana.

'Excuse me, Ma'am,' he said eventually. 'Forgive me for asking, but just how long have you been smoking such large cigars?'

'Well, Mr Vice-President,' came the drawled, if hesitant, reply, 'If you must know, ever since my former husband found a half-smoked one on the bedside table.'

By the way, it was Spiro Agnew who was described as the only American politician with real convictions – which he had, for fraud.

Humour and wit swirled easily around on the sidelines of public life, especially when the central character has become a legend in his, or her, own mind, and the surrounding acolytes relieve the tedium or the tension by creating their own world of ridicule. And ridicule is what the majority of politicians fear most. David Steel has made no secret of the fact that his image as a small puppet in David Owen's pocket, in the *Spitting Image* television programmes, did him more than a little damage. Particularly effective in destroying someone is the snigger, wink and nudge reaction every time a certain person's name is mentioned. Sir Clive Sinclair, a gifted inventor, has said how he hated the ridicule far more than the technical criticisms, when he launched his electric car. Among many classic examples from my time at the Palace was one about the Leader of the Opposition in New Zealand, who went on television to criticise some aspect of The Queen's visit there. David Lange, the then Prime

Minister, made the journalists laugh when he said that he always sought a second opinion – from a taxidermist – about anything his rival said. It killed his opponent's criticisms stone dead.

An American ancestry and frequent transatlantic visits have stirred a life-long interest in the language and customs that bind and separate the United States and the United Kingdom. As with the other subjects in this book, this issue also has to do with the perceptions we have of each other, largely as a result of the mutual television images we have thrust upon us. We are not two nations: each is several, with different habits and obsessions, differing ways of laughing at different things, and eating in different ways. Anything we believe about the other is likely to be true and equally likely to be false. Even if we think we know the United States, our knowledge tends to be shrunk and pigeon-holed, with a lot of trivial visual images of broad-brimmed hats, motels, yellow cabs, blue-rinsed old ladies, shrinks and incompatible tastes mixed up on one plate. I still remember with great joy watching that outstanding and indefatigable Private Secretary to The Queen, Sir Philip, now Lord Moore sitting down with great relish to a huge breakfast of crispy bacon and eggs in a hotel somewhere in Wyoming, and, as he was about to set to work on it, a helpful American waiter pouring a generous helping of maple syrup over the lot.

Americans' perceptions of themselves further complicate matters. Sinclair Lewis put it well when he said, 'intellectually, I know that America is no better than any other country; emotionally, I know that she is better than every other country'. No matter who is president, there is a fundamental and implicit belief that America holds the world together. Because Americans are a melting-pot of races, they also thought, until recent tragic events intruded, that they understood the outside world, though Jimmy Carter, who did for peanuts what Reagan was later to do for jelly beans, in an unusual demonstration of wit, likened his nation to a bowl of uncooked minestrone, where the individual bits had never entirely merged.

The last time I met President Reagan was during a visit he made to London shortly after he left office. I heard him speak twice in the course of two days. The first was at one of the famous American oil company dinners arranged by that incisive journalist and television interviewer, Kenneth Harris. Two hundred of the great and the good were there at Claridges to hear the former President – but the speech was a disaster. As he advanced on to the podium, Reagan dropped his text on the floor and the pages got mixed up as he retrieved them, so he lost his way several times, to the embarrassment of all. He did not seem to have any staffers there to help him, something that would not have happened in Mike Deaver's time. The next day, when Mr Reagan spoke again, it was without text or notes, at a Saints and Sinners lunch. He was a changed man, and had us laughing to tears and clapping all the way through, as he regaled us with fine anecdotes of his Hollywood days.

EIGHT

Household Duties

All ceremonial is ridiculous unless it is perfect.
Lord Cobbold

Ten years of births, marriages, divorces and deaths: the mystery of the monarchy that Bagehot wrote about came with the smell of fresh paint that accompanied every royal visit, at least that is what it always felt like. It rode side by side with the split identity of the tabloids, which, to quote the *UK Press Gazette*, were seemingly intent on 'licking the royals to death'. Arriving not too many years after Court correspondents had to turn up for their briefing meetings in tailcoats, I, too, had to have something of a split identity at the Palace, to keep abreast of reality – hard-working Marks and Spencer's day clothes, and a wonderful velvet-collared Household tailcoat by night, that had originally been made for some superannuated general, back in 1903.

My father always used to warn that proficiency at snooker was the sign of a wasted youth, but one member of the modern monarchy gave the lie to that view. When The Princess Royal recently visited Saughton Prison in Edinburgh, among other parts she went to was the youth wing and its whitewashed recreation area, where, surrounded by a wall of warders, a handful of ill-favoured youths were playing a desultory game of snooker. No way were they going to do anything but stare with hostility, or show a total lack of interest in their royal visitor. A small but memorable scene ensued. Princess Anne picked up a billiard cue from a rack, and started potting the balls with considerable expertise gained from years playing the green baize at Sandringham and Balmoral. The youths' admiration broke through and they began to talk animatedly with her until her programme forced her departure. They smiled, shook hands warmly, and waved as she left.

It is easy to forget that Princess Anne was attacked and almost kidnapped in the Mall in March 1974. Her police protection officer at the time was the cool and fully collected Aberdonian, Jim Beaton, who eventually became The Queen's own protection officer. The story of how he won his George Cross, and the details of his heroism, have often been told. He was shot several times by the assailant, and ended up with a punctured lung and many months in hospital. But, at the time, as he gradually sank on to the roadway and into unconsciousness, he told us that his only Aberdonian thought was 'Hell, this is a brand new suit, and look at the holes in it now!'

At the Palace, as the communicator with the outside world, I was to realise, early on, that you may have a message, you may think it clear and clearly expressed, but unless it gets through and is fully understood, then the exercise is a failure. The story of the Lord Chancellor of the time, Lord Hailsham, well illustrated the point. One day, after lunch, he was progressing through the Central Lobby in the Houses of Parliament, in all his ceremonial gear, full wig, robes, knee breeches and silk stockings – the lot – to take his place on the Woolsack in the House of Lords. He was preceded, front and rear, by the ornately dressed Officers of the House, a fine sight in any circumstances. The Central Lobby was, as always, crowded with MPs, their constituents, and lots of Japanese and other tourists, watching open-mouthed at the process of modern British democracy at work. Lord Hailsham recalled that he spotted his friend, Neil Martin MP, standing to one side of the Central Lobby, so naturally he raised his hand and called out 'Neil!' Inevitably, many Japanese tourists, and others, had to be prised from their knees.

As a first public communications duty of any substance, during my second week at the Palace I had to announce, and field questions about, Princess Margaret's divorce from Lord Snowdon. But a stranger duty in that line came in 1978 when I had to try to understand the arcane workings of the Roman Catholic Church in their annulling Marie-Christine von Reibnitz's previous marriage to a British banker, Mr Tom Troubridge, before she could marry Prince Michael of Kent. I had known something about that branch of the family, for while in the Foreign and Commonwealth Office I had shared an office with Prince William of Gloucester until shortly before he was killed in an air crash in 1972. But on marital matters, just try explaining to your average tabloid journalist why someone should then be known as Princess Michael, when you did not fully understand it yourself.

I had seen the cult of personality, or hagiography, at close quarters in both Ghana and Romania, and it was not pleasant. In Britain there is a strange dichotomy as regards the royal family. Marshalled by the media, its individual members go up and down in popularity, a flux seldom anything to do with the individuals themselves: sometimes they can do no wrong, sometimes no right. The Queen and other members of her family have walk-on parts in other people's lives. But they are not actors and actresses in a soap opera; they are real. They really do go around switching Buckingham Palace or Holyrood lights off to save money. I remember the latter particularly, since who would dare switch back on a light that The Queen herself has extinguished, even if it means stumbling one's way through some of the spookiest rooms in that Scottish Palace, to one's bedroom just next to the one with the brass plate on the floor where Darnley, Mary Queen of Scots' lover, was foully murdered?

The Queen and her family have their jobs for life – they cannot retire – and press secretaries at the Palace have to cope with that fact. The story has been told elsewhere of my buzzing The Queen on my ancient intercom one day, to tell her that I had just heard on the radio that The Queen of the Netherlands had abdicated in favour of her daughter.

'Typical of the Dutch', came the brisk reply. No room for doubt on that subject.

When things became tough, a press secretary felt like the rubber between the door and the door frame, when the wind of public opinion, stirred up by the media, came along and slammed it shut. Coping with that reality was hard at times.

A small domestic scene erupted when I returned home after my very first overseas State Visit, taking in Saudi Arabia and four or five of the Gulf States. On these tours there were a number of young footmen in the party, because members of the Household, who might only get a few hours' sleep a night, still had to look smart and tidy when with The Queen. So the footmen did a certain amount of ironing and packing, and checking luggage and so on. I eventually arrive back in the bosom of my young family, unpack, and, in a moment of inattentive irritation, exclaim: 'Damn it, my footman's forgotten to pack my toothbrush.' It was not a remark that went down well in domestic Pimlico. Modesty was always a useful watchword, and so, when, after the wedding of the Prince and Princess of Wales, I found myself talking to a group of three men at the reception, then realised that they were all ex-Kings, Michael of Romania, Simeon of Bulgaria, and the most impressive of them all, King Constantine of the Hellenes, I kept the story to myself when I returned to domesticity.

Protocol and etiquette, the oft-mocked handmaidens of power, were of some importance at Buckingham Palace, but we constantly saw how much they mattered elsewhere as well: 'Only fools mock etiquette' – Talleyrand again. Slights were given, and grave offence taken, not just over where someone was placed at a State Banquet, but also in a reception line, a theatre, a restaurant, or at a wedding breakfast. The ranking of individuals, by themselves and by others, is a fascinating study.

Working at Buckingham Palace gave plenty of opportunities to reflect on such things, for instance, on whether The Queen might take offence when her lady prime minister turned up at a function in a royal blue dress. Of such themes were tabloid headlines constantly manufactured. An attempt to make out that such stories were in some way in the 'public interest' was and is an argument which the media uses to justify their more dubious activities, when what they are usually talking about is 'the public's interest', which is a very different thing. Everyone loves gossip, the little inside stories, and we are particularly good at bearing with equanimity the misfortunes of others, especially those who hold high office. It interests us enormously, but the 'public interest' justification is usually wafer-thin.

No amount of spindoctoring can improve on certain realities. The first half of 1982 was, for example, a trying one for the British government, between Argentina invading the Falklands on 2 April and their surrender on 14 June. Memories of these events are blurred except for the fact that I had, in the brief absence of the Duty Private Secretary one night, to inform The Queen of the loss of HMS *Sheffield*, before she heard it on the news. Her response was a uniquely understandable silence.

Buckingham Palace added to the government's problems at the time, with the incident in which Michael Fagin entered The Queen's bedroom on 9 July, and Her Majesty was a pool of calm in the subsequent pandemonium, a characteristic further displayed when blanks were fired at her as she was riding on horseback down the Mall to the Trooping the Colour. Then there was the sad and over-hasty dismissal of Michael Trestrail, her loyal personal protection officer, over the weekend of 17/18 July. Looking for someone to blame, and hounded by a baying press pack, the government of the day, and especially the then Home Secretary Willie Whitelaw, used a series of ill-designed sledgehammers to crack the resulting hornets' nest. The story was told about Willie Whitelaw that Margaret Thatcher had said to him, 'Willie, the trouble with you is that you agree with the last thing anyone says,' to which he had responded, 'I agree, Margaret, I agree.' His dismissal of Trestrail proved just that.

But that was then. Who was my first ever royal? In my childhood days, I was cycling back to school after an afternoon of sports somewhere in the north of Scotland, when I got a puncture. I had no puncture kit with me. It was a long way to walk for a small boy. A large car pulled up. A man, two men, got out. They shoved my bicycle into the back of the car, and gave me a lift to school. It was only afterwards I was told that one of the men was the Duke of Edinburgh. I was very young and far from sure who the Duke of Edinburgh was. I did not think about the royal family for a quarter of a century thereafter. Much later in life, when I told him, the Duke, hardly surprisingly, confessed he did not remember his rescue of a small and insignificant schoolboy.

Ten years of life attending events with The Queen and other members of the royal family highlighted the fact that, through no fault of Buckingham Palace, hundreds, if not thousands of people had spent hour upon hour waiting for them to arrive. It was always the local organisers who insisted that schoolchildren were up at crack of dawn, that girl guides and boy scouts, tiny cubs and little brownies, stood for unnecessary hours waiting for The Queen to pass by. The greatest dignitaries, lord mayors, lord provosts, lords lieutenant, chief constables and civic worthies of various sorts put themselves, equally unnecessarily, in position long before the royal party was due to arrive. On a surprising number of occasions, The Queen's cavalcade would have to wait, perhaps in a lay-by, careful not to arrive too early, for that was a most grievous fault.

On one never-to-be-forgotten occasion outside Wells Cathedral, the royal party arrived a few minutes early for a Maundy service. Those sitting with The Queen in the royal Rolls were convulsed with laughter since, across the heads of a sea of people waiting to greet her, five or six mitres and croziers could be seen bouncing along above them, as a phalanx of bishops ran from the door of the cathedral to the place where the royal car was to stop. It was something Monty Python could not have invented, as the bishops ran, holding their vestments high above their feet, to avoid tripping. The monarch took some time to compose herself, and we deliberately blocked the press cameras from seeing her, since it might have been somewhat unseemly for her to meet her bishops with tears of laughter running down her face.

One evening The Queen drove back from a private visit to the BBC, having previewed the material specially shot for inclusion in a Christmas broadcast. She travelled, with only a discreet police escort, in the small Rover she used for such private journeys, so we got stuck in a traffic jam along the Bayswater Road. We stayed there for some time, with no one passing by on the pavement noticing the distinguished occupant of the car, until a large black lady, perhaps a childminder, for she was corralling five or six multicoloured children along the pavement, noticed that it was indeed The Queen. A huge beam of a smile, and then, one by one, the lady picked each child up and held it close to the window, at a distance of only eighteen inches, to wave at The Queen, who carefully waved back to each one in turn.

I recall another traffic jam, this time with the Prince of Wales, coming down Park Lane just past the Dorchester. It was one of those gridlocks that looked as if it would remain solid for some time to come. With us in the royal car was Cliff Morgan, the former Welsh rugby international, and by then the Head of Royal Liaison at the BBC. The Prince, late for his next appointment, decided that we would all get out and walk. The police escort did not like that sort of thing, since it had not been long since the IRA had killed guardsmen and horses nearby in the notorious Hyde Park bombing, but walk we did.

Outside the Hyde Park Hotel, a group of Welsh tourists spotted Cliff Morgan, and, to the Prince's amusement, immediately surrounded him, demanding his autograph, totally ignoring, and not even recognising, their own Prince of Wales. Cliff was embarrassed, but, as always, too polite to push past, and because of police anxieties, unable to tell his fans who they were ignoring. He tried to gesture to the Prince to go on, and that he'd catch up. No way: the Prince was enjoying it all too much, particularly the wonderfully Welsh remark from one of the fans: 'I saw you on the wireless yesterday, Cliffy'.

When we finally got away from the fans and walked back to the Palace, Prince Charles remarked to us, a trifle wistfully, that he had not walked that way, nor even through that part of Green Park, since he was a child.

Births, marriages and deaths. Enough has been written about the first two, and divorces are not for here. But two images of death I will describe. I was mowing the lawn at my house in North Berwick on 27 August 1979. It badly needed cutting, because it was my job and I had been away at the Lusaka Commonwealth Conference, followed by a lengthy African tour. On the previous evening we had played a hard game of croquet well into the night, and, as the light failed, a poor little hedgehog, which had rolled itself into a ball in the long grass, had been mistaken for one of the balls by a friend who was visiting us. The hedgehog, unhappily, did not survive. There was even less happy news to come.

As I was mowing the lawn, my elderly mother appeared at the door telling me that Buckingham Palace wanted me urgently on the phone. I was used to urgent phone-calls, but it was still to be a full five years before I got my first mobile telephone – one with a huge battery, like a small box of bricks and just as heavy – to lighten my task. That pleasant sunny day, as I had only another twenty minutes or so to go before I finished my task, I told my mother to tell them to ring me back later. A few minutes later, they rang again. Again a message was sent back: nothing could be that urgent. When they rang a third time, I switched off the mower, and, cursing under my breath, took the telephone call. Lord Mountbatten had been assassinated, blown up by the IRA while steering his fishing boat, *Shadow V*, out of the little harbour of Mullaghmore, in County Sligo.

Lord Mountbatten was a man with the greatest presence, not least when dressed in full uniform to ride beside The Queen at the Trooping the Colour. He also had an incisive mind, which I constantly saw echoed in the character of the Duke of Edinburgh. I remembered seeing him on the *Johnny Carson Show* in America, long before I went to the Palace, sometime during the Vietnam crisis. He had warned Carson that, given his long military experience in South-East Asia, and as Viceroy and last Governor-General of India, he was absolutely not going to comment on American policy in that war. Despite that, Carson slipped in a question, on the lines of what would he, Mountbatten, do about Vietnam if he were the American president? Quick as a flash, Mountbatten replied, 'I'd tell the British to keep their noses right out of it.'

One possibly apocryphal but conceivably true story of Mountbatten is of his being confronted by his local Tory parliamentary candidate, who had come round canvassing before a general election. Mountbatten is alleged to have said, 'Actually I'm a Labour supporter, but I think my butler votes Tory.' His biographers have spelled out some of his vanities and weaknesses, particularly in rewriting his place in history, but that history has always been forgiving. As Philip Ziegler revealed at the end of his measured biography of Mountbatten, after expressing his frustration with the character of his subject, he had felt it necessary to place a notice on his desk as he was writing which read, 'Remember, in spite of everything, he was a great man'.

Mountbatten had already planned his own funeral, but the manner of his going made it all the more majestic and poignant, something he would probably have appreciated. As for me, when I heard the news, I was on a special flight to London within the hour, and I never did finish mowing my North Berwick lawn.

The other funeral, clearly remembered, was that of the Duchess of Windsor at St George's Chapel, Windsor. One brief moment afterwards comes to mind: Queens in black veils watch the departing coffin, then, to one side, by the wall of the chapel, two mourners, like ghosts from a long-forgotten past, the Mitford sisters, Diana, who had married Sir Oswald Mosley, and Deborah, the Duchess of Devonshire.

One funeral that was not to be until many glorious decades later than expected was often speculated over, particularly when Charlie Douglas-Home, the then editor of *The Times*, personally rang up one Monday morning to say that he had heard, on the very best authority, that The Queen Mother was at death's door, and could I please check. Editors of *The Times* did not ring me up every day, and as he had said he was so sure about his source, I decided to check it out, since I was not always aware of what went on in Clarence House. I rang The Queen Mother's exuberant old Private

Secretary, Sir Martin Gilliatt, a man of whom it was said that his job fitted him 'like a prawn in aspic', who listened quietly to my hushed tones, and then replied 'Michael, you may tell your journalist friend (journalist? The editor of *The Times*!) that he, I'm glad to say, has his facts wrong. Her Majesty has, at this precise moment, got her waders on and is up to her waist fishing in the river.'

Stories of Queen Elizabeth The Queen Mother, and particularly her dining habits, are legion. How many of them are true is another thing, but having known the lady and worried about things like the press coverage of fish-bones getting stuck in her throat, and given the laughter and fun that always surrounded her, all yarns are possible. (Incidentally, for fish courses, there was no special fork and knife at Clarence House, only two forks, an old-fashioned but very manageable Victorian alternative.) It was said of her father-in-law, King George V, that when a guest at his table drank by mistake out of a fingerbowl, the King followed suit so that the guest did not feel he had done anything wrong. The Queen Mother's solution, when someone made the same mistake, was to turn to the guest and say sweetly, 'Oh don't worry. The Archbishop of Canterbury did just the same thing last week.'

Another true story was of her being told by a worried member of her Household, during a private visit to France, that at lunch that day she would have to sit beside the local mayor.

'So?', The Queen Mother asked.

'I'm afraid he's a communist, Ma'am.'

'Oh good. I do so love communists', came the disarming reply.

Finally, Queen Elizabeth herself told me the delightful story of how, at the end of the Second World War, there had been a concert at the Palace, and Louis Armstrong had been invited to come to play. Before one number he looked across at the King and said with his huge grin, 'Now this next one's for you, Rex!'

Until the cross-party political vandals of Britain's international prestige took away the royal yacht, disembowelled and emasculated it and put it in its new setting of Leith, The Queen took particular pleasure in her Western Isles tour on *Britannia* each autumn.

Official visits were paid and received in remote communities, giving much pleasure to both sides. On the days off, the usual routine was to find some deserted beach and have a lunch-time barbecue, irrespective of the weather. The Duke did the barbecuing on his personally designed barbecue, while The Queen made the salads. After lunch it was either serious cleaning up the beach time, and burning or taking away the litter and flotsam of the years, or going for a good hard walk.

One inclement day, The Queen, in headscarf, dark glasses and mackintosh, led the walk, with a lady-in-waiting, a policeman and Shea for company. We had landed on a small, deserted – we thought – island, just to the south of Colonsay, and we set off to walk right round it along the shoreline.

On the far side of the island we saw, approaching us, a family of four: the husband, the wife and two small girls. We waved a greeting and then stopped and chatted to them. They were from Glasgow, and had permission from the farmer who owned the island to camp there for the week. My walking companion was not recognised.

The wife had exciting news to impart. Did we know that the royal yacht was anchored off the other side of the island? Yes, we did.

'It looks very handsome, doesn't it? We're wondering why it's anchored here. Wouldn't it be fun if . . .', all this in broad vernacular.

At that point in the conversation, the younger of the two little girls, a child of around seven, looked closely, pointed upwards, and said, in broad Glaswegian, 'You're The Queen. You're The Queen.'

'That's me,' came the response or something like it. The family looked suitably stunned, but then took it surprisingly well. We onlookers, including, I noted, the policeman, found it all very emotional. The Queen played the part to perfection, and even agreed to pose for a photograph with them, provided, please, that it didn't end up in the next day's tabloids.

Was it that evening on the yacht that I was reminded by a very persuasive Princess Margaret, who had been tipped off by a disloyal fellow member of the Household, that I knew the words to a couple of Scottish republican songs, learned in my student days? One went:

Nae Liz the One, Nae Lizibeth the twa,
Nae Liz shall be oor queen,
For ho can we hae a second Liz
When the first yin's never been.

Another verse went as follows:

Noo her husband Phil's a bonnie churl,
But he's one o' thae kilted Greeks,
Oh he may think that he's the man,
But it's her that wears the breeks!

I was handed an extra whisky to toast my daring, and went to bed, waking up with a sore head and panic in my breast. The P45 must be on its way. But much laughter was my reward: it was always like that.

This sets the scene for a brief tirade about scuppering the royal yacht. From the moment it was first seen, sailing in all its glory up the East River off Manhattan, with millions lining the banks to watch, I recognised, in terms of perception, what a terrific ambassador it was for Britain. It was used not just by the royal family, but by many a trade delegation, promoting the best of British in overseas markets. And because of the perception the world had of it, and Britain through it, even though it was getting a little old-fashioned, everyone was attracted to it. All the great and the good came. No one turned down an invitation to dine on board. Those politicians, of both parties, who destroyed it when the monarchy was at its weakest, should hang their heads in shame. They would not have dared to do it, as I write this, in The Queen's Golden Jubilee year.

Just as countries need symbols to identify them, so do corporations and individuals. By your outward signs are you known, fat, slim, tall, short, bald, toothless. On that last point, I know a very able man whom few take seriously, simply because of the absurd nature of his teeth. They are an orthodontist's paradise of shapes, skewness and lack of proximity to their molar mates. When this man talks, we do not listen but stare in wonderment at how he could possibly manage to chew his food, let alone brush his teeth. A recent study by researchers at various British dental schools involved taking photographs of subjects smiling, before modifying the images digitally. 'Before and after' pictures were shown to a group of 200 people, and where the teeth appeared discoloured or decayed, the subjects were universally deemed to be less successful, have a lower intellect, and much poorer career prospects. Margaret Thatcher recognised this decades ago, not only in having elocution lessons, but undergoing extensive corrective dentistry.

There were no problems on that score when Lady Diana Spencer came on the scene. So much has been written about her that it would be pointless for me to add anything, but for one insight. It has been said by many that she was not trained, shown the ropes, or told what to expect when she first came to Buckingham Palace in 1981. That is simply not true. We took her to newspaper offices and television newsrooms, and arranged that she even listened in, or, on occasion, actually answered journalists' questions anonymously, by sitting in the Palace Press Office and taking calls. We rehearsed her early speeches, and her answers to formal interview questions. When she and the Prince were to be interviewed by Andrew Gardner and Angela Rippon – and she was most reluctant to be interviewed by the latter – each question, we promised her, would be prepared in advance. Diana had no wish to be as sharp as her stepmother's mother, Barbara Cartland, who was much on the news at the time, basking in Diana's reflected glory. Interviewed on BBC Radio Four's *Today* programme, she was asked whether she thought that the class barriers in Britain had at last broken down.

'Yes of course', came the incisive reply, 'otherwise I wouldn't be sitting here talking to people like you.'

But the future Princess of Wales's vulnerability was always there, particularly in the last months before her wedding. Crossing Vauxhall Bridge in the back of an official car with her one day, I was laughing at a story of hers, about how she had just tousled the hair of a small boy who had been standing on the edge of the crowd, waiting for her.

'Why aren't you at school?' she had asked him.

''Cos I got sent home,' he grinned. 'Teacher says I'm crawling with headlice.'

Suddenly the mood changed, as the Princess-to-be looked up and saw a huge hoarding, advertising some newspaper or other, with the banner headline screaming 'Diana – the True Story'. She collapsed on the seat beside me, crying that she just could not take it. And that was before her marriage. There are many versions of the truth about the meeting of editors that I called to discuss the problem of her being harassed by the press, but that comes in its place later.

There always was a lot of laughter, even in the tensest of times. It was always so. The story goes that King George V was talking to a very left-wing Labour MP at the time of the 1929 Stock Market crash, asking him if he thought things were really as bad as the press were making out.

'Yes, Mr King,' came the reply. 'They are. If I were you, I'd put the Colonies in the wife's name!'

Laughter was also used to lard tact when Lord Snowdon gently wondered, when he was taking a formal photograph of The Prince of Wales and Diana Spencer to mark their engagement, whether he, because he was rather shorter than his fiancée, might agree to stand on a box. Laughter again after filming The Queen's Christmas broadcast one year, and she agreed, as a memento, to be photographed with Richard Cawston, the director, and the rest of the BBC film crew. Some time later she met Dave Gorringe, the sound operator, and asked him if he'd had the photograph framed yet.

'Yes, Ma'am, but it cost us all a real packet.'

A look of royal astonishment.

'Yes. First we all had to go round to Harrods to buy silver frames for them, and then get a grand piano each, to put the photographs on!'

NINE

Princes and Potentates

Counterfeit values always resemble the true.

W.H. Auden

In the management of perception, State Visits, incoming and outgoing, are seldom, if ever, given much attention by the media, unless they are controversial. When Lord Mountbatten refused to take part in the ceremonies surrounding the visit of the Japanese Emperor because of his own bitter wartime experiences in the Far East, the press found out, and there followed a great deal of excited coverage of that so-called snub. State occasions are finely crafted symbols, but they can have serious political significance, as President Ceauşescu of Romania and his advisers recognised, which is why they pressed the British government so hard for an invitation. Ceauşescu demanded this type of recognition from the West, and my experience of such occasions is that we need to look hard at the leaders of other countries before condemning our own.

By pure chance, the first inward State Visit I had to handle when I was appointed to the Palace was indeed that of the Romanian President and his unbearable wife, Elena. Most of the pre-visit negotiations focused on what British honours were to be bestowed on her, and although in the end there were none, one university was bullied into giving her an honorary degree. I made the brief mistake of speaking in Romanian to the visiting journalists who had accompanied the President, and the next day, the party newspaper in Bucharest, *Scintea*, announced that The Queen had specially appointed a Romanian-speaking Press Secretary in honour of her distinguished guest.

Even before the President's arrival, the Romanian advance party had been difficult in the extreme. They seemed to demand that Buckingham Palace be redecorated to suit Madame Ceauşescu's colour preferences. In reality, the hardest of the hard men in that advance team, the President's head of security, Ion Pacepa, who later wrote up the story in his book *Red Horizons*, was secretly arranging his own defection to the Americans at the same time, but that we knew only later. When the whole party arrived, what did happen was that the Securitate guards did their best to prise off the gesso and gilt panels from the walls of Buckingham Palace, and nearly destroy the chandeliers in search of British listening-devices. We later warned the Americans, who were also due to host the Ceauşescus, to nail down any valuables, and screw the paintings to the walls, to avoid them 'going walking' on the President's departure.

The Romanians were not unique. Sadly, even when every invitee to a Palace function was a household name, little things would go missing as 'souvenirs'. On one famous occasion, at the end of the Second World War, King George VI gave a magnificent dinner for the victorious allied generals and admirals. The gold plate was all returned to Buckingham Palace from the caves in Wales or other secret hiding-places, where it had been stored throughout the war. At the end of dinner, the guests were standing around in the State Rooms with their coffees and brandies, when the King noticed an American admiral, with a dozen rows of medal ribbons on his uniform, quietly slip one of the monogrammed, silver-gilt coffee spoons into his pocket.

The King summons Mr Churchill, and tells him what he has just seen.

'What do we do, Prime Minister? It will quite spoil the wife's cutlery set.'

'Leave it to me, Sir,' says Mr Churchill.

He paces slowly over to a side table, and, picking up the largest serving spoon he can find, sticks it into the breast pocket of his dinner-jacket, with the bowl of the spoon in full display. He then goes over to the admiral and says, 'It's no use, Admiral. We've both been spotted. We'll have to put them back.'

On a happier note, some of the best gifts given and received on state occasions were not the things of silver and gold, but the symbolic ones, with that special personal touch. I remember seeing a tear glistening in the corner of the eye of the otherwise hugely self-contained and cool President Mitterrand of France, whose family symbol was an oak, when he realised that the young oak trees in their oaken tubs that he was being given came from Windsor Great Park and were the very personal choice of his hostess.

Generally speaking, outgoing State Visits were more fun, much more hard work, and had dangerous undertones, though the management of the perception of them was often difficult. During the early eighties the press had, at times, to be encouraged to cover them at all. Those that related to Commonwealth Heads of Government meetings were definitely not a switch-on for the tabloids, with Kelvin Mackenzie the editor of the *Sun* admitting to me that, 'as soon as I allow the word Commonwealth to creep into a story, I lose 99 per cent of my readers'.

The task that sticks unhappily in my memory from Commonwealth meetings was the apparently simple one of getting forty or fifty heads of state and government to pose for the group photograph. With the Duke of Edinburgh briskly chiding me for not getting them into the right places in time, as they fought, oh so courteously, for precedence to stand in the front rank near The Queen, pushing a barrow filled with frogs would have been easier. Then, orchestrating the groups from a position between them and the photographers, the Duke would yell, to the delight of my loyal friends in the press pack, 'If you want to be a power behind the throne, Michael, get behind the blinking throne.' Such is gratitude.

The climate on an overseas reconnaissance visit, made in advance by three or four members of the Palace staff to prepare

The Queen's programme in detail, could occasionally be an indicator of things to come. I have a photograph of myself, taken in New Delhi, standing beside a ferocious-looking Sikh who was one of the personal bodyguards to the Indian Prime Minister, Mrs Indira Gandhi. I was told later that it was almost certainly the very one who assassinated her in 1984. During the visit itself, I hardly recognised the Indian Prime Minister at first, when I stood by her side, sheltering from the rain outside some conference hall, for she was dressed very simply in a headscarf and brown gabardine raincoat. I remember that indomitable lady remarking that she was 'just enjoying the rain', then later relating to me a remark, made by her famous namesake, Mahatma Gandhi, that 'All the world would be Christian, were not Christians so unlike their Christ', which recalls George Orwell's equally telling accusation that the 'worst advert for socialism is its adherents'. Another little story of hers concerned the Mahatma going to Buckingham Palace before the war, to meet King George V. On leaving he was asked by the press whether he had felt in any way ill at ease, having only been wearing a loincloth. 'Oh no,' he replied quietly. 'His Majesty was wearing enough for both of us.'

And another quotation springs to mind when remembering that humble-looking woman, Mrs Gandhi. Her father, Jawaharlal Nehru, the first Prime Minister of an independent India, memorably said something that many world leaders forget to their detriment: 'We are but little men, serving great causes, and only because the cause is great, does something of that greatness fall upon us also.'

One favourite Indian story, passed on to me by the cricketing hero Denis Compton, told of his sitting one lunch-time in the reception area of his Calcutta hotel, since the Test Match had been rained off for the day, and noticing a small Indian bellboy in a turban, holding up a little board with bells on it, on which his name had been chalked. He called the boy across and asked what the message for him was.

'Oh Mr Compton, Sir. This is your early morning call, Sir,' came the carefully defined reply.

But then what is time? We crossed India by train, staying overnight in a splendid imperial coach. We had that day's local newspaper when we boarded, and, amazingly, the following day's when we appeared for breakfast the next morning. Two dates, but the same newspaper.

One reconnaissance trip to one of the more remote islands of the Pacific led to a few of us being entertained to breakfast, under an awning on the beach, by the prime minister of that tiny realm. He asked whether we liked fresh coconut milk, and when we replied in the affirmative, he stood up from the immaculate breakfast table, took off his shoes there and then, and climbed to the top of a huge palm tree in his bare feet – no branches, remember – and threw down a couple for our refreshment.

On another Pacific trip, I had it reported to me that Colonel Rambuka, in his published memoirs about his attempted *coup d'état* in Fiji, had called me one of the most ethical and diplomatic people he had ever met, and also that I was 'very nice', as if these attributes could not coexist. I never normally reject undeserved praise, but if, in that tropical paradise, my memory lingers on, it is entirely one-sided. I have no memory of ever having met Colonel Rambuka.

Then there was the diplomatically testing reconnaissance trip we made to prepare for The Queen's visit to the Shah of Iran. It was, unbeknown to us, just before the revolution that would sweep him from power, but we got as far as Bander Abbas, an untidy naval dockyard town in the south, before we realised that, almost certainly, the trip was not going to happen. For appearances' sake, however, we had to continue to act as if it was, so we negotiated about this and that, as was usual in such circumstances. For example, we indulged in empty debate over The Queen's wish to travel in a glass-topped Rolls-Royce so that the people could see her, and at a speed, say, of five miles an hour, rather than in a black-windowed Mercedes with many police outriders, screaming through the streets at ninety, which was the normal progression rate of the powerful in that part of the world. Everyone we dealt with was naturally unsettled by events, not least the Shah's nephew, a naval officer, with whom I was meant to be dealing on press matters. I got more than a bit annoyed with his lack of attention, until a member of the British Embassy staff whispered to me that he was rumoured to be about to cut and run for asylum in the United States.

I could hardly blame the man, since I had been particularly impressed, at another meeting that day, this time with the local chief of police, when we asked him whether he was worried about the recent riots and other imminent signs of revolution in the capital, Tehran. He merely shrugged, smiled, and then stood up and went to a framed photograph of the Shah that was hanging on the wall behind his desk. He carefully turned it round on its hook, and showed us that, on the back, he had sellotaped a photograph of the grim Ayatollah Khomeini.

Once our visit was over, we made to leave our nervous hosts, board the Andover of The Queen's Flight, and fly home. But we could not do that. Despite being official guests of the government, we had not had immigration department stamps put in our passports when we arrived, so we could not be allowed to depart. Many angry hours later, a compromise was reached. Arrival and departure stamps were put into each of our passports simultaneously. Not surprisingly, The Queen's visit never took place.

I was never happy during our reconnaissance visit to Saudi Arabia, a country led by members of its huge royal family, but largely run by expatriates, from the European professionals at the top, to the Palestinian or Egyptian middle managers, to the poor Filipino servants at the bottom of the tree. This was in the late seventies, and The Queen, when she came, was, in the walled garden of their minds, to be welcomed as an 'honorary man' – their phrase – because she was Head of State. 'But, Mr Shea', said the Minister of the Court coolly, 'No female journalists, please.'

In that marvellous marble palace, full of elegantly white-robed and bearded protocol officials, I chose my battlefield with care, explaining, courteously, I hoped, that, in my view, it would be totally impossible to ban female journalists from travelling out to cover The Queen's visit. If we tried to stop them, which we would not even think of doing, the resulting media outrage would mean that the whole visit would be put in jeopardy, indeed it would probably not take place. I urged a rethink on the part of the Saudi government. I would, horror of horrors, even try to get agreement from those female journalists accredited to the royal visit, that they would dress appropriately: no trousers, long dresses, arms and heads covered, and so on. Privately I shuddered at the thought of my trying to police a dress-code for such a determinedly feminist group, at least two of whom were already rumoured to be going to write a book about women in Muslim society, given the special access they were hoping to have as they followed The Queen's visit around that forbidden kingdom.

There was an outburst of sudden anger, then a long debate. Then more anger. The place of women in different societies was aired, recognised, and set aside. After much heart-searching and telephoning to the religious authorities, appropriately dressed women journalists were reluctantly to be allowed to cover the visit.

Then came the matter of 'The King's Clemency'. As a mark of appreciation, on the occasion of the British Queen's visit, all British subjects in Saudi jails – there were about a hundred of them at the time, almost all in prison for alcohol-related offences, which of course are serious crimes in that Arab country – would be released, pardoned in the name of the King's excellent majesty and generosity.

We said how thankful we all were. It was a most magnificent gesture.

Our deliberations completed, the Minister of the Court, a Saudi prince himself, clapped his hands, and two tall, very black servants in very white servants' uniforms appeared instantaneously.

'Drinks!' said the prince. 'It has been a most productive meeting,' or words to that effect. 'Now what would you like?'

The servants opened a wall cupboard to reveal one of the most well-stocked bars I have ever seen. That famous bar on the island of Skye could not have boasted a greater range of malt whiskies, not to mention the gins, the brandies, all the wines and spirits in the world. And why not? There are double standards in every walk of life.

I remember only one failure of humour, again during the Saudi trip. We had lunch in the desert, in a great tent, seated on rich carpets – a stunning medieval scene, eating lamb and rice with our fingers. The *Evening Standard*'s cartoonist, Jak, captured the scene exactly, except that The Queen's place is empty, and a row of dots indicates her rapid exit from the tent. A turbaned waiter is bending low over her place, holding a roast on a silver platter. His head is turned towards us and he is saying, 'But I thought she liked corgi!'

The cartoon is faxed, with other press cuttings, to the royal yacht. I show it to the Duke and others. Roars of laughter. 'Show it to The Queen too,' he suggests. I am vaguely aware that they are watching me closely as, beaming happily, I so do.

The Queen looks briefly, then turns away. 'I don't think that's at all funny,' she says, eliciting roars of laughter from the spectators behind me.

Two other culinary images remain with me. That banquet in the Saudi Arabian desert took place without me. Not that it mattered, because, as the senior guests stood up to leave the meal, more junior members of the tribe took their places in order of rank, until, at the end, the servants came to consume what remained. I ate nothing that day in the desert, for I had seen the silver salvers piled high with rice and lamb, lying on trestle tables outside, waiting to be served inside the great tent. At least I thought it to be rice and lamb, for everything was covered in a thick mat of black flies. I invented an urgent press briefing I had unexpectedly to give.

During a civilised banquet later on in that same visit, I sat opposite the most famous Saudi of the day, Sheikh Yamani, arbiter of the world oil prices, controller of Saudi Arabia's oil wealth, master of all he surveyed. To one side of him sat The Queen's doctor, Professor Norman Blacklock, an amusing and kindly man in every way, known always by the Duke of Edinburgh as Hemlock, and who, thankfully, was almost never needed on tours, except to treat the tummy upsets of the travelling British press corps. He and Sheikh Yamani spent most of the meal talking, not about critical world issues, but about the merits of different types of bran for the digestive system. Professor Blacklock is a urologist (favourite joke: never accept a drink from one!) and the dietary benefits of bran were always of consuming interest to him. In the middle of their conversation, Sheikh Yamani turned his attention to me. There were three large glasses at each place setting round the table. No alcohol of course, but one for sparkling mineral water, one for a rather pleasant yogurt drink, and one for surprisingly refreshing ice-cold camel's milk. Dreaming of a cold beer, or perhaps a long gin and tonic with ice clinking in the glass, I had been imbibing quite a lot of camel's milk, and Sheikh Yamani had noticed. He insisted that from then on I should drink equal amounts of the milk and the yogurt drink, 'Otherwise, with the milk's richness, Mr Shea, the consequence will be dire.'

I did as directed and all was well for me, but Norman used up almost his entire stock of tummy pills on the rest of the unsuspecting Household over the next few hours.

There were always problems with meals. I got into trouble twice in Dar es Salaam in one day. Harassed after a late morning briefing meeting with journalists, I arrived late for an official lunch, and slipped into my allotted place beside a nice young man with a North American accent. He failed to introduce himself, but we chatted pleasantly enough. After lunch, I was accosted by a Canadian journalist, whom I knew slightly, and asked what I had thought of my table companion. In my haste, I failed to note the elephant trap, and remarked that he seemed nice enough, but that he appeared to be completely out of his depth, and that I was not even sure he knew he was in Africa. Back in Canada, my remark about the newly-appointed Canadian Foreign Minister hit all the headlines.

There was more to come that evening. The Queen was accommodated in a guest palace, while the rest of us were in a pleasant modern hotel in downtown Dar es Salaam. I was shown into my room on the eighth floor, and, as I entered, I saw, jumping down from a low coffee table, three or four rats that had been nibbling at the bowl of fruit left out for me. The rats ran off out of the French windows on to a small balcony, and disappeared.

That night, after dinner, I had a drink at the hotel bar with some British journalists, who were always looking hungrily for a new story, like crocodiles round a canoe. A whisper travels faster than a shout, and they paused in their chatter as they overheard me asking the passing German hotel manager how on earth rats had got up to the eighth floor of his hotel. The journalists loved it when he replied, 'They don't. They come down from the restaurant on the ninth floor!'

Oh how we all smiled, until I heard about the front-page story in the next day's London *Daily Telegraph*, where the accident-prone Press Secretary to The Queen was being chided for laughing at the expense of Tanzanian tourist facilities. I had to apologise once more, though the habits of the rats of Dar es Salaam were hardly my concern. A touch unfair, but that sort of thing came with the job.

Was that where one rather short journalist, let us call him Harry, made some familiar remark to a very tall woman journalist, let us call her Anne, to the effect that he would like to f . . . to make love to her? Anne looked all the way down from her eminent height to Harry, standing well below her. The response was, to say the least, effective. 'Harry, if you do, and I ever find out about it, I shall be very annoyed indeed!'

The position of The Queen in her role as Head of the Commonwealth frequently created headlines that had more to do with perception than reality. This was further complicated by the fact that she was, at the time, Head of State of sixteen or seventeen different countries, and that the government of these countries had no inbuilt need to agree with each other on matters of foreign policy. Rhodesian sanctions overshadowed much international debate in the late seventies and early eighties, yet I remember how she took it totally in her stride when in February 1983, as Queen of Jamaica, she had to make a speech from the throne to her Jamaican Parliament, in which she roundly condemned the actions and policies of Her Britannic Majesty's government. It is a schizoid role demanded of few, as is her task of being Head of the Church of

England, and the expectation that as soon as she crosses the border, without any complaint or religious soul-searching, she worship with the Church of Scotland.

As Head of the Commonwealth, The Queen was believed, and I do not know what her true feelings were, to be much more supportive of the Commonwealth majority and the United Nations when it came to the question of sanctions against the illegal Rhodesian government of Mr Ian Smith, than was the then British government, led by Mrs Thatcher. Things came to a head at the Lusaka Commonwealth Conference in August 1979, which The Queen and her advisers knew she had to attend, despite the fact that a guerrilla war against Smith was being waged by the Patriotic Front of Nkomo and Mugabe. Would The Queen be safe, was the question of the day. From whom should she take advice? From the government of the United Kingdom, or from those of her other realms and territories? The Queen went to Lusaka, and, for her decision, there was nothing but praise in the world's press. This is no place to develop the ins and outs of what happened thereafter, but suffice it to say that she made it very clear to the African leaders gathered there that while she would never be drawn into a political argument about Rhodesian sanctions, thank you very much, she could play a role in diffusing tensions and getting the opposing sides to speak to each other. Indeed she did play a part in encouraging the more extreme leaders to get their newspapers to advocate negotiation rather than recrimination, and to look for solutions rather than pursue differences. This is no secret, for her admirer ex-President Kenneth Kaunda, among others, has talked openly about it since, recording that the positive outcome of that conference was in great measure due to The Queen making her views on compromise known to all concerned, and particularly to the African leaders who held her in great respect. Another stalwart for compromise was the hugely perceptive Prime Minister of Singapore, Lee Kuan Yeu, whose opening speech to the Conference was outstandingly accommodating, and it too helped set the tone of the occasion.

This image of The Queen as conciliator was widely reflected in the local press. A press cutting from one Zambian newspaper excitedly declared that she 'could easily be elected Queen of the World', while Malcolm Fraser, the Prime Minister of Australia, wrote of her actions that it was a high point in Commonwealth history.

That was not a one-off. Later, visiting Tanzania, accompanied by President Julius Nyerere, the latter said openly to The Queen, after a spectacular day when the crowds came out to cheer her in their hundreds of thousands, that if she ever decided to return and stand for the presidency, he doubted, if he dared stand against her, that he would gain a single vote. Much laughter sealed the mood on these occasions, for there was no doubt that these African leaders, in particular, genuinely admired and respected her. Later, in press briefings, it was made clear that The Queen's position as Head of the Commonwealth could no longer be seen as a colonial hangover. There was no need to add that there was a new and lively perception of her role, for even the most cynical of the London broadsheets reflected just that.

Thus it was that, after the successful Lancaster House Conference, the Prince of Wales travelled out to Rhodesia in 1980, and, at the stroke of midnight, on 17 April in Salisbury, the new state of Zimbabwe was born, the forty-third member of the Commonwealth. For me personally, it was an amazing few days, taking me back to that night in the Resident Clerk's flat in the Foreign and Commonwealth Office, when UDI was first proclaimed. The characters were great too – the African leaders, but also Christopher Soames, the larger than life last Governor; and, throughout, the heady presence, as adviser and friend (or was he perhaps just the weaver of his own dreams?) of Laurens van der Post. Travelling out on the Prince's plane with us, when he was not with his host, he sat throughout that long flight, telling my assistant and me the most marvellous stories, or magic fantasies, of Africa and the world he had known. Whether his own records of his role in bringing about Rhodesian independence, through influencing everyone from Mrs Thatcher to the Prince of Wales himself, are true or false – and he has had his many detractors – they were among the most beautifully, no, hauntingly told stories I have ever heard. And what is the truth except what one believes to be the truth? Van der Post, above all, believed in them.

Another continent, another time, another scene. I found no aping of Western cultural niceties nor presentational diktats in China. Picture the scene: The Queen and the Duke of Edinburgh are sitting in wickerwork easy chairs beside the ruler of China, Deng Xiao Ping. We are outside in the gardens of the presidential palace, within the high-walled leadership compound, close to the Forbidden City. We are drinking tea. Deng is smoking, and no harm in that. A spittoon is a good two metres away from him. He uses it with the greatest of accuracy. The Duke lets out a guffaw of amusement and admiration. The Queen's face is expressionless. She sees but does not show it.

This was the China of a State Banquet in the Great Hall of the People at which there were twenty-three courses, with goldfish swimming about happily in little pools in the middle of the tables. Other fish were less lucky: for one course, live fish were shown to each guest, dropped straight into boiling oil, then flipped out crisp on to our plates. Such banquets are more than meals, they are great occasions, where, especially in Beijing, the challenge was in identifying what had been placed in front of one, beautifully presented and dolled up like a rookie politician on his best behaviour. Washed quickly down, as it had to be if it was something best left uneaten, with quantities of rice wine, which lightened the heaviness of the conversations, these feasts would have left you hungry if you had expected British-style sweet and sour pork with chicken-fried rice.

This was also the occasion of the Duke of Edinburgh and the 'slitty-eyes' affair, a brilliant example of how when certain 'truths' take hold they become almost impossible to shift. Let me screw down the coffin lid on that story once and for all.

It happened like this. The Queen and the Duke of Edinburgh are visiting a university in China. The Duke meets, among many others, some British students who are studying there. We are standing in brilliant, dazzling, sunshine. 'How long have you been here?' he asks a Scottish student, eyes half shuttered against the sun.

'About two years, Sir,' or some such answer.

'If you stay any longer,' says the Duke, eyes continuing to squint into the sun, 'you'll get slitty eyes too.'

No harm in that, you'd think. Then a journalist, who wasn't even in on the conversation, asks the student what they talked about. The student tells him. The journalist naturally expands on the story when he tells the others in the press pack what he thinks has been said. The press universally file their pastiche of a story that the Duke has called the Chinese slitty-eyed.

That evening, at the daily press conference, the Chinese Foreign Minister is asked if he has taken offence at what the Duke said.

'No. Why should I?' comes the bewildered reply.

'Surely this is a gross insult to the Chinese people?' asks another British hack.

'Certainly not!' The Foreign Minister cannot understand the fuss. And so on. The story sticks. Who can argue with dozens of identical stories, filed by journalists, none of whom was actually there?

In my experience, press officers of all persuasions try to help the media get their stories and transmit their film and stills. On another occasion, during The Queen's visit to Shanghai, there was to be the most wonderful picture opportunity – almost as good as the one arranged for them on the Great Wall of China.

A pretty Chinese teahouse stands on a little island in the middle of an artificial lake, connected to the mainland by a traditional, willow-pattern-style, arched bridge. The Queen and her host are to walk over it together. They would, I promised, pause at the middle for photographs. Those inexperienced in such matters do not understand what is involved in a huge press shoot like that. For walkabouts, something the press called the Sheamobile was constructed from a flat-bed trailer, towed by a tractor, on which a stand was built to give the photographers a raised position, moving slowly before The Queen, to cover her progress. This time a static tiered scaffolding stand has been constructed, at great expense and trouble, to give every one of the hundreds of TV and stills cameramen a splendid vantage point, from where they would have their few brief moments to record such a picturesque occasion. Every last one of them is deeply grateful. This, after the one on the Wall, is to be *the* photograph of the entire trip. The scene is set.

At the last moment, in front of my unbelieving eyes, a large detachment of Chinese soldiers, security men and police march in between the several hundred-strong media pack and their view of the pretty little humpbacked bridge. As you can imagine, Shea loses his cool, flails his arms, shouts, argues, tries to push some of the security people aside, even into the lake if he could. The media are furious, but they love it too. Back home, Shea is the lead item on the evening TV news. Photographs of him going bananas are on television and every front page the next day. 'Shea takes on Red Army', is the *Guardian*'s banner headline. The Queen's visit takes second place. And I was just trying to help.

There were several happy visits to other kingdoms; those to King Hussein of Jordan and King Olav of Norway particularly come to mind. I had first had to deal with a problem relating to King Hussein in the early seventies, when I was in the Foreign Office on the Middle East desk. The King was in London for secret meetings with the Israelis, and, as he had been the subject of many assassination attempts, his security was paramount.

The British government's ban on handguns being carried by the bodyguards of visiting VIPs was absolute, but not quite. King Hussein was a little different, and a blind eye was turned, until one of his bodyguard's revolvers went off accidentally while his convoy was passing across Lambeth Bridge. No one was hurt. The disinformation system sprang into action. Despite rumours to the contrary, the noise had just been a car backfiring, as they frequently did in those far-off days.

The King took personal control of the visiting reconnaissance team when we arrived to plan The Queen's visit to Jordan. For a brief stage of the drive, on the way from Amman to Petra, I sat in the front passenger seat, with the King beside me driving his own bullet-proof Mercedes. Bullet-proofing means a very heavy car to drive, and I commented on his road-handling skills. He talked about the many other features of the car. I asked what the strange handle beside the steering wheel was for, and reached to indicate what I was talking about.

'Don't touch it, Mr Shea,' said the King sharply. I was well warned: it was a James Bond device – a machine-gun or something like it, built in under the headlights, to deal with a potential ambush on the road ahead.

Later, learning that I was Scots, he told me how much he liked to go up to Argyll on the west coast each autumn, when he could.

'Not always the best time for the weather,' I remarked.

'But you have to understand: I go there for the cool and the rain,' he replied, 'though you can keep your midges.'

Everyone liked King Olav of Norway. A great contemporary of Queen Elizabeth, The Queen Mother, 'Onkel' Olav had been born at Sandringham, as befitted a grandson of Queen Victoria. Even in his seventies and eighties, he would go off skiing on his own in Norway, without any security protection. 'Why do I need any? I have four million body guards,' he would say, referring to the whole population of Norway, where he was hugely popular, even with that country's few republicans.

In old age the King would fall asleep, even while someone was talking to him, but then he would wake again after a few moments, full of life and vigour. Once, on board *Britannia*, I asked him how – he had once been an Olympic yachtsman – he still lived such an active life, and he responded by calling over his military equerry who was standing by the door, clutching an official-looking leather briefcase.

'Open it and show Mr Shea,' he said.

The equerry, slightly abashed, did so, to reveal among various papers, several pairs of carefully folded black silk socks.

'Change my socks four or five times a day,' the King said. 'That's the secret.'

A rather special bilateral State Visit to Norway, and then to Orkney and Shetland, took place in the early eighties. I particularly remember the reconnaissance trip because I was seated in the rear of the British Ambassador's car with The Queen's Assistant Private Secretary, Robert Fellowes, outside the Munch Museum in Oslo, when a call came through from Buckingham Palace, to tell Robert that his sister-in-law, Diana Spencer, was about to get engaged to the Prince of Wales. The call also instructed me to come back to London on the next available flight, as I had to arrange the press announcement.

Later, after a most successful visit by The Queen to Norway, King Olav embarked with us on the royal yacht *Britannia*, and set sail for Orkney and Shetland, two groups of islands that had, for centuries, been part of Norway. A day or so later, when about to begin a walkabout among the crowds outside St Magnus's Cathedral in Kirkwall, The Queen turned to the King with a smile and said, 'You go first. This place is as much yours as mine.' Everybody laughed. If only all territorial claims could be dealt with so magnanimously.

The marvellous friendliness and the space of Canada, a sort of America as if it were run by the Swiss – this was my impression following a mind-blowing, whistle-stop train tour across that continent. We stopped at one small town after another, sometimes for ten minutes, sometimes for an hour, with flag-waving children everywhere, scouts and guides, old folk in wheelchairs, every corgi in the nation, and the local mayor in his chain of office to meet and greet, with the immaculately controlled Canadian Mounties and the snow-topped mountains always in the background. There were innumerable lunches, always in the largest covered space available, always with prawn cocktails to start with, and rubber chicken to follow, meals that were difficult to spoil for hundreds of fellow guests, and difficult to enjoy when eaten time after time after time. Much of the work on that trip was taken off my shoulders by my soon-to-be Canadian deputy, the broad-shouldered Vic Chapman, who had worked for Pierre Trudeau, and who handled the travelling press corps with the skill and strength expected of a former star with the Edmonton Eskimos, even when it meant throwing them out of The Queen's path.

'I saw you throwing that photographer aside,' she said to him on one occasion.

'Oh no, Ma'am, I'd never do that,' came the gentle reply. 'I just picked the man up and kept walking.' The photographer should have known better: there is a famous picture of Vic holding a young Marilyn Monroe outwards and upwards in the palm of his outstretched hand.

But from one Canadian trip, apart from the singing of their moving national anthem 'O Canada', I vividly remember, one night in the late seventies, after a long and tiring day, that the Prime Minister, the ever-youthful Pierre Trudeau, suggested to Prince Andrew, who on this occasion was accompanying The Queen, that the two of them might now go on to a nightclub and dance. Separated by this time from his wife, Margaret, Trudeau, according to the press, had a vibrant relationship with a beautiful Canadian Olympic athlete, but that was none of my business. I was tired, since I had spent much of the day denying that the Prime Minister, who had been finishing a holiday in Morocco with the lady in question, had caused any offence to The Queen by not being there to greet her when she first arrived in Canada.

Shea is just getting into his pyjamas and is looking at his bed in great anticipation when there is a knock on the door. What do you do when you are in your pyjamas and dressing-gown, and your monarch is standing there and telling you about an unexpected nightclubbing adventure?

'Keep it out of the press,' I am told by my bed-heading Household colleagues, as I get dressed again, 'otherwise it will wipe The Queen's own trip off tomorrow's front pages.'

I commandeer a car and a police protection officer, find out where the wayward Prime Minister and Prince have gone, and force my way into the nightclub. By this time the young man is on the tiny floor, dancing with ten pretty, and pretty excited girls, all at once, and someone has, of course, telephoned the newspapers.

I am the killjoy. I bark out my instructions. No press are to be admitted or the Prince leaves. Perhaps ten minutes elapse. I hear, above the wild music, the banging on the doors, the cries and pleas, and offers of bribes to the doorman, from without. I go up to the door. Through a gap, I see twenty or thirty crazy paparazzi outside, and is that a battering ram they have found from somewhere? I find myself pleading with the Prime Minister of Canada and with a Prince. I am not a popular chap, but we make our escape through the kitchen entrance, and, with no photographs to go on, The Queen dominates the morrow's headlines.

A host of other impressions spring to mind, from a myriad other visits. I recall The Queen being mobbed while trying to walk down Wall Street in New York City, where we, the Household, had to link arms to force a way through, since all the cops were too busy taking photographs of her. That was the visit when The Queen drove the wrong way up Fifth Avenue in an open-topped limousine, and then through part of Harlem, something no American president of the time would have been allowed to do. The huge crowds on the way caused the *New York Post* to abandon its usual 'Headless Body found in Topless Bar' style front-page banner headline, in favour of 'Manhattan's a British Isle today!'

Another occasion meant having to give up the idea of a walkabout in Rome, because the press pack became totally unmanageable. That visit to Italy I remember for two incidents: one, on the reconnaissance, when we visited a palace, and twenty of us in the party burst through the double doors from one ornate room into another, to see the young dukeling of the house dallying, in flagrante, with two nubile young housemaids. Later, when The Queen went to the ruins of Pompeii, the vigilant Italians had carefully stuck sheets of brown paper over the more explicit brothel murals, so that the royal party would not be shocked – some hope! – or perhaps so that the paparazzi would not get photographs of the distinguished visitor with a salacious bit of vintage porn behind her.

There are other happy and unhappy glimpses from elsewhere: my being spat at, full in the face, by some unwashed anarchist during a very civilised visit to Zurich; or the memory of rows and rows of elderly women, lying silent and soundless under iron-sharp, white linen sheets, in the Hospice de Beaune. Then there were those other old ladies, almost unrecognisable as Europeans in their Chinese clothes, British ladies who had lived in China all their eighty or ninety years, through wars and revolutions, pulled out of the past to attend the garden party held by the Consul General in Shanghai for The Queen in 1986. When she tried to talk to them, one or two of them needed an interpreter. We could understand that, but not what they must have gone through across the years.

Fame has its uses. The night I announced that I was leaving the Palace and moving on to another life, the press tracked me down to where my wife and I were having a birthday dinner with David Frost and David Steel, at a fashionable Beauchamp Place restaurant. I had no wish to speak to or be photographed by them, so the two Davids kindly created a diversion, by going outside and talking to the press, while we slipped away into the night.

TEN

All Sorts and Conditions

All men are born equal, but quite a few get over it.
Lord Mancroft

Age equalises everything. Remember the story of the 83-year-old Clemenceau, passing a pretty girl in the Champs-Elysées? 'Oh to be seventy again!' he said with a sigh. The anecdote reminds me of the famous lines:

A man is not old when his hair grows grey.
A man is not old when his teeth decay.
But a man is approaching life's long sleep,
When his mind makes appointments his body can't keep.

I had toyed with the idea of having a chapter of this book entitled 'Courtesans I have known', or *Les Grandes Horizontales*, but too many problems of a legal and social nature have deterred me. I am a reasonable man, I think, and the reasonable man adapts to the world's rules. The unreasonable man changes things. Fame is the final stage before the fall. Only a tiny number of individuals have lifelong fame. How many living former British prime ministers or American presidents are there? Who really remembers Diana now? Monarchs are different: they have the job for life.

Sitting on the sidelines, it has been particularly fascinating to watch two groups of people, their habits and peculiarities. One group are the social élites, the people about whom I have been writing in this book, and the other are the famous. Often they are one and the same; sometimes they are very different. I could write endlessly about the little old American lady, a widow who cruised a great deal on the QE2. She always booked three of the most expensive state cabins on the ship, one for herself, one for her maid, and one for her dresses. Or perhaps I could reminisce about the American industrialist, Armand Hammer, whom I met frequently when he chased around after the Prince of Wales, a man who claimed that he made his first million dollars while still at medical school in the 1920s. He may have been the dynamic head of the Occidental Oil Corporation, with wonderful connections as the go-between with the Soviet Union, but all I remember were his legions of staff who were there to record his every doing, to photograph and record them in writing and have them leather bound in a new volume by the end of each week. The élite are a mix and mingle of those members of the Establishment whom I discussed earlier. While the famous can be our rulers, they can be famous merely for being famous, if they sit at the glitzy end of the social spectrum.

'We are all born equal,' said the late Lord Mancroft, 'but some of us manage to get over it.' Putting it another way, we all end up leading or being led. The Chinese talk about the 'Mandate of Heaven', which means, quite simply, that legitimacy in government is conferred by the simple proposition that if one contestant for power proves the stronger, then the Mandate passes to him, which says much for the practicality of that race. In sociological or social anthropological terms, élites in any society, the effortlessly superior, have a specific role as the leaders of a clan or tribe. It is politically incorrect to give too much weight to such terms in modern democratic societies, with the word 'élitist' often becoming a term of tabloid-style political abuse, like the word 'art' or 'artistic', with its overtones of exclusive upper-class attitudes and behaviour. What élitism should mean is all to do with good taste and excellence, along with genuine merit, but that argument, for the moment, is lost.

Setting aside those who are born into the élite, like the British royal family for example, and presuming that the old aristocratic families have more or less had their day, there is still no doubt that in the United States and much of Europe, members of certain families, who speak with the same accents, go to the same fee-paying schools, wear the same ties, shop in the same shops and go to the older universities, tend to end up in the top jobs in many of the professions. This is even more the case in Africa, Asia and, above all, in the Arab world, where a dynastic system – when it works – of replacing monarchs or tribal chiefs can often help with an orderly succession when the current holder dies. Elsewhere in life, decisions as to who takes over when the boss retires or is sacked are often messy affairs, with many good warriors being slain on the way. One of the problems is of course that just because you are well born, and are 'one of us', it does not mean that you have any talent. I am not reflecting here just on Britain. Look, for example, at President George W. Bush; would he be where he is if his father had not trodden those boards before him, and does it much matter? For, in such cases, a group of managers and aides springs up ready to help do the job. Like membership of the Establishment, the door to élitism is always open, but it takes certain Darwinian skills to push through into a bigger room.

Fame is a different matter. Elites run things, but, outside a small group of their peers, members may not actually be famous, in that the media give little or no attention to them, nor ever proclaim their power and influence. I have known four Secretaries to the Cabinet, who many people in government would agree are among the most powerful or influential men (they have all been men so far) in Britain, but, except for a small burst of excitement by a few political correspondents in a few broadsheets when they are first appointed, they can seldom be categorised as famous. Not one in a thousand British people would recognise their names, and even Lord Rothschild, when he joined the Cabinet Office in the seventies, remarked, 'Until this week, I never realised that the country was run by two men I had never heard of' – the other doubtless being either the prime minister's private secretary or the permanent under-secretary at the Treasury.

I have used both the words powerful and influential, but they are very different attributes. Power, which Bernard Shaw called 'the ability to achieve intended effect', is a pretty rare thing. Absolute power, thank God, is shackled by so many constraints, and while the so-called powerful may be able to buy obedience for a while, that is usually the end of it. It has been widely recognised by historians that in modern America one of the last people to have more power, and for longer than any other political figure, was J. Edgar Hoover, the former director of the FBI, who served under no less than eight presidents. On occasion, he would personally lead his G-Men, who were trained in the 'machine-gun school of criminology', on shoot-outs with whoever was currently Public Enemy Number One.

I have heard J. Edgar Hoover speak. I was a student on a summer working scholarship in Springfield, Massachusetts, one week of which was spent on an organised, getting-to-know-Washington week. My host that day was a young official whose job, he told me, was to 'get people like you to love America', that being one reason for the scholarship. I was shown round the Senate and the White House, and then, in the late afternoon, taken to a large hall, whose name I forget, where the speaker, addressing a huge audience of civil servants of one sort or another, was Hoover himself. Do I remember what he said? No, sadly I don't, but I recall the atmosphere of awe and certainty in that room, and the lengthy applause that followed his every remark, just as the communist faithful applauded Ceauşescu's four-hour speeches.

The trappings of power are often just as effective as the reality. I have seen famous men become tongue-tied in the presence of the monarch, and a much-medalled general become almost incoherent when introduced to President Reagan. The crowns, the robes, the court dress, the startling tunics of the military equerries, or the smart suits and the efficient charm of the courtiers or private

146

secretaries, the pomp and circumstance of protocol, even the secret service men with their earpiece communications and dark glasses, make the strong meek and the meek tremble.

Let me tell two stories, the first of a famous governor of one of Britain's most notable colonies, coming to be knighted by his monarch and being told precisely what to do at the investiture in the ballroom of Buckingham Palace. The Lord Chamberlain explains, with infinite patience, that he is to walk in front of The Queen, bow, move a couple of paces forward, kneel on the stool with head slightly bowed, then The Queen will use her father's sword to tap him lightly on the shoulder, and award him the accolade of knighthood. He then stands, is briefly talked to by The Queen, bows, and backs away. This poor man gets as far as the stool when, in his tension, his knee locks in position, and he has eventually to be carried off by two footmen, his foreleg jutting out behind him.

Yet another remembered occasion features a new Lord Mayor of London. He is in a complete sweat about his forthcoming investiture, so the Comptroller from the Lord Chamberlain's office takes him through the routine as above, but then sees that, in his panic, the man is taking nothing in. So what the Comptroller finally says is 'Look, old chap, don't you worry about a thing. Just do what the man in front of you does.'

Unfortunately that normally super-accurate courtier had forgotten what everyone at the Palace knows, which is that you don't always do what the person in front of you does: in my day, one in every five men in the receiving-line to shake hands with The Queen, if it was a husbands and wives occasion, would do what the person in front, of them did on such stressful occasions, and give a slight curtsey.

On this occasion, the man in front who was also about to get a knighthood, is the native Governor-General of some remote Pacific island, whose custom is to greet his monarch by doing an elaborate and lengthy war dance, with much hand-clapping, and sticking out of tongues, before getting down to the equally arcane process of being awarded the accolade. Memory does not recall whether the poor Lord Mayor rose or sank to the occasion.

Power is one thing, influence another. 'All rising to a great place is by a winding stair', said Francis Bacon, and that process continues to this day. Without calling them conspirators, though I have called them 'influents' in the past, I have seen many such figures rise through almost unnoticed routes, their influence on events scarcely discernible even by those closest to them. In most societies, the top is very small and the ante-rooms, filled with a miasma of the influential, are also tiny, for power is never what it seems, and responsibility is not power. The influential come from many and varied backgrounds. They can be advisers, strategists, private secretaries, but they can also be spouses, mistresses, lovers, chauffeurs and hairdressers, and in case you think I am joking, I knew one very famous businessman who discussed his every move with his personal valet. Influence at work can make a fascinating study. It ranges from a whisper in a prime ministerial ear to a letter to *The Times*, but to be effective, it has to be employed at the right moment. I remember listening in on one conversation, where a prime minister said aloud that she, guess who, could not think whom to appoint as the chairman of one of the greatest corporations in the land. Someone fairly low down in the ranks, who just happened to be standing beside her, came up with a name, and the appointment was made within the week.

The most influential man in my early Whitehall years was undoubtedly the huge presence of the late Lord Goodman, who on some minor issue while I was in the Cabinet Office, when I was talking above my rank across a meeting-room table, took the time to take me aside later and say, 'Remember the chess Grandmaster called Tartakower? He famously said that the mistakes were all out there waiting to happen.' Then he went on, 'You don't need to rush things, and push your own view too soon, Shea. Learn to sit back and watch others play their hand first. They're quite likely to play a wrong hand, then seize your chance.' He said just that, and that precisely: I know, because, unusually, I wrote his words down straight away.

While to *Private Eye* he was 'the abominable Goodman' or 'Goodmanzee', the *Guardian* called Goodman the 'universal fixer', as befitted a man who served on countless quangos, was Chairman of the Newspaper Publishers Association, and the most successful of all Chairmen of the Arts Council. Harold Wilson once wrote that he 'helped the system work when it wasn't working'; but while Goodman was known to be sympathetic to the Labour Party, Edward Heath also asked him to help bring about a settlement in Rhodesia. The latter summed him up thus: 'He knew all the people and did all the work', which, from Heath, was praise indeed. At boring meetings, I collected some of Goodman's expressions, such as 'If I may say so . . .', or 'Far be it from me to push you to take a decision . . .' and then he would do precisely that.

The only person I met who could rival Goodman, apart from the Law Lord, Lord Denning, who long championed the rights of the individual (his favourite subjects were, he said, bureaucracies and deserted wives) and some of the top civil servants of the day like Robert Armstrong, was Sir David Napley, who was never averse to taking on a difficult or unpopular client. I spoke with him on a platform on more than one occasion, and his tight legal mind and dry wisdom were always apparent, though, because he was so devastatingly clever, his enemies saw something sinister in his professional clarity.

At the time I had dealings with GEC, the Chairman was the former politician, Lord Prior, and while statements at their annual general meeting might have appeared to emanate from him, every serious decision was taken by the man who had really run it for decades, as its managing director, Arnold Weinstock. He had an aura of power about him, as did Tiny Rowland, which was partly to do with the deep awe in which their immediate staff held them. But beyond that, what is this ephemeral thing called fame, and why are we, the people, attracted to it? What does it mean to be famous, where your name is everywhere except in the telephone directory? Does fame really mean working on becoming well known, and then wearing dark glasses to avoid being recognised? Is the only ingredient of fame the column inches of coverage and the minuteage of airtime?

When I was in the public eye because of the job I was doing at the Palace, it would never have occurred to me to think that I was famous. If I was, it was merely reflected. Fame is when you are recognised wherever you go by people in the street. I remember two giggling girls in a lift in Harrods, asking me if I was who they thought I was. I replied that it depended who they thought I was, since I am constantly mistaken for a great Welsh actor. (I fail to see the similarities myself.) Fame, quite simply, is this: we are invited to an amazing summer party every year by David and Carina Frost, and everyone there is a well-known face. I recognise them all but myself. They are all photographed by the paparazzi that crowd around the gate. You know fame by the number of camera flashes as the guests arrive. Fame used to mean having a statue made of yourself and put upon a plinth after your death. No living person has a statue made of themselves (a bust maybe), just as no living person is represented on a postage stamp or banknote apart from the head of state. Sorry, I forgot: there is a well-known statue of Lady Thatcher, but it keeps being decapitated, which is a lesson for us all.

Fame and the famous. People gravitate towards them because they exist, perhaps for that reflected glory, perhaps because they think that something special will be imparted by them. In practice, in my experience, most of the famous have very little to offer anyone, nor are they overburdened by any particular qualities.

There are exceptions. I remember a certain spring day in 1956, while I was doing my national service in Germany. I was sent off to the American Zone on some long-forgotten attachment, and, as I stepped off a train in Munich, I was greeted by a screaming throng of young women. There were thousands of them, stretching into the far distance, filling every corner of the station platform. I had to force myself, and my army kit bag, past them. The thought that this might be some sort of welcome for me was soon dashed. I looked along the train and saw someone half poised, half stepping down from the high German passenger train: it was Elvis Presley, in full US military uniform, hair black and Brylcreemed in the afternoon light.

Another miniscule glimpse of fame, and of another station, came later that same year. In London King's Cross I saw two people standing waiting for a train, two people I knew I recognised. I smiled at them. I went up and naïvely said hello. They asked how I was. I went on my way. Once on the train I saw a newspaper photograph: Richard Burton and Elizabeth Taylor had returned my greeting pleasantly enough. Later, when I met the latter at the British Embassy in Washington, she admitted to me that she was far from happy having stolen the television lights away from the monarch. She was said to have had an on-off relationship with Princess Margaret, who, on one famous occasion, remarked on the vulgarity of the enormous diamond ring Miss Taylor was wearing. Dame Elizabeth slipped the ring off and persuaded the Princess to put it on her finger. 'There,' she said. 'Doesn't look so vulgar now, does it?'

A host of other memories stand crowding round the door to the past. The one marked theatre for instance, has, as well as Burton and Taylor, Noël Coward in the seat in front of me, a young eagle (*un de mes faucons* – i.e. *faux cons*), by his side, talking noisily through a bad West End play. And there is A.E. Matthews, well into his late eighties, with the audience on the edge of their seats, laughing with him, but waiting for him to forget his lines or dry up, as he did so much towards the end. On stage the telephone rang – was the play *The Chiltern Hundreds*? – and Matthews dried, then picked up the phone, and addressed the only other actor on stage with the words, 'It's for you.'

A few feet away Marlene Dietrich is singing, in the early sixties at the Lyceum in Edinburgh, a theatre of which I am now the Chairman. I was in the second row of the stalls, so close that her décolletage was revealed as a skein of fine, skin-coloured silk, that stretched cleverly, in wrinkle-free camouflage, from low-cut dress top to the choker around her neck. But God did the hairs on the nape of my neck stand out when she sang 'Underneath the lamplight, by the barrack gate . . .'. I heard her singing later, in Berlin, but they never really forgave her there.

151

Another face by that door recalls a night at the long club table at the Garrick, where members, dining alone, may sit where they wish. I am so fascinated listening to the High Court Judge on my left, who has spent the day sentencing IRA terrorists for life, so he can't just go home until his police or special branch minders arrive to escort him there, that I failed to recognise, until almost too late, that other very modest man, Alec Guinness, seated quietly to my right.

'Oh no. The judge has far more interesting stories to tell than me,' said Sir Alec, when we chatted briefly over the cheese and coffee.

Three more views from the sidelines. One, a porter from our apartment block in New York, pointing to an elderly, nondescript lady passer-by and telling me in a whisper that it really was Greta Garbo. Two: taking the lift from the floor below the penthouse of the Rembrandt Hotel on Park Avenue, New York, I step inside to find it is already filled with a small round man, a huge cigar, and clouds of illegal tobacco smoke. The cigar is taken and replaced between the lips with the hand and fingers holding it, in an instantaneously recognisable way, from underneath.

'Good morning, Mr Burns,' I say politely. Who could not, alone in an elevator with the legendary American comedian, George Burns?

He removes the cigar from his mouth once more, holding it in the air in front of him, looks at me, smiles, and returns my greeting, adding, 'I'm always glad when the day starts this way. It proves to me I'm still alive!'

A third: a big nineteenth-century railway station, at Rolandseck on the Rhine, once used by the Kaisers as a point of departure for the hunt, long abandoned, and now restored as an arts centre. We had great parties there, and one memorable concert, where I stood by a wrought-iron gallery beside a lady of a certain age, listening to Yehudi Menuhin play. Afterwards, I introduced myself to her as a diplomat from the British Embassy in Bonn. 'And you?' I hesitate.

'I . . . I am just that fiddler's moll,' she replied.

Another early memory is of a literary party held in my student flat above a pub in Rose Street in August 1962, during the Writers'

Conference which was part of that year's Edinburgh Festival. When I bought the flat for the huge amount of £800 in 1959, it had a small, barred, speakeasy door in the door, though it had not been used as a drinking den but as a brothel. The flat's notorious past was not mentioned when I relinquished my flat for a week or so to accommodate, as tenants, Colin MacInnes, author of the definitive novel of swinging London, *Absolute Beginners*, and the famous or notorious Norman Mailer, who had shocked the world with his book, *The Naked and the Dead*. After Norman left Edinburgh, and a couple of books signed to me as his 'absentee landlord', he also left a telephone bill which amounted to the, in those days, enormous sum of £120, as a result of lengthy phone calls he had made to his then wife, Lady Jean Campbell, in New York. These were the heady days before he was arrested and charged with stabbing her, and indeed before he ran for election as the city's mayor in 1969. It took months for me, or rather the conference organisers, to get my money back.

One night, during the conference, we had a party. I saw William Burroughs sniffing white powder up his nose, and when I asked about it, I was told it was a kind of snuff. We were all innocents in those days, and drugs were almost unheard of. Late that night, the police invaded the flat. I remember a bluff police sergeant watching curiously as Burroughs sniffed some more powder, then he turned and gravely told us all not to drink so much, and to keep the noise down. We were disturbing the neighbours.

Drink was a constant companion, to be sure, in those days. Mailer had an altercation with the translator of Boris Pasternak's *Dr Zhivago*, and the latter fell or was hurled down the stairs of a flat in Edinburgh's New Town, while, on another occasion, my Rose Street flat became a field dressing station, when Jim Haynes, who founded the Traverse Theatre, brought a blood-soaked John Calder, the famous polymath and publisher, to be washed down after a skirmish involving a bottle and Sonia, George Orwell's widow, in a little Greek restaurant across the road.

There was another party, this time in Glasgow, and five of us crammed into a tiny car for the forty-mile drive home on the twisting A9. No motorways in those days, and the party had been so well fuelled that it took me time to discover that the little lady who sat on my lap in the back seat all the way – she was pretty heavy by the end – was Muriel Spark, who was very much in her prime. Or another journey, with David Steel driving, taking the drunken and rumbustious James Robertson Justice and Compton Mackenzie back from a debate in the Edinburgh University Union to the latter's house in Drummond Place, and us immature young chaps being quite astonished at the vulgarity of these two distinguished figures as they tried, in their whisky-befuddled state, to insert a key in the front door. 'If it had curly hair round it you'd get it in, laddie,' et cetera, et cetera.

In such a literary environment, where, as editor of the University revue, *Gambit*, I had just published two new poems by Yevgeny Yevtushenko, I began a lifelong interest in creative writing – which has so much in common with spindoctoring. I had read that Somerset Maugham had argued there were three rules for writing but that unfortunately no one knew what they were. I had smiled at Disraeli's alleged remark that 'when I want to read a novel, I write it,' and when reading that Churchill had warned that writing began as an adventure, then became an amusement, then a mistress, then a master and, finally, a tyrant. Later I realised the truth of all this. Writing was a profession or occupation, and, if you were published, no one thought you ridiculous even if you never made any money. Hemingway was good on the subject too. 'The best training for a writer is to have had an unhappy childhood,' and then, later, he added that the successful should begin by 'taking the juice from two bottles of whisky . . .'.

The joy of communicating through writing fiction is that you play God and do not have to be truthful. You can create the nastiest characters, and then disown them and their opinions. But, like spindoctors, you have to use every method of persuasion so that lies become as vital as the truth. Your characters, to misquote Nabokov, are like galley slaves, while you stand on the bridge with a whip. The most deceitful words have to convince. And they have to convince publisher, critics and readers too. No author is a genius to his publisher, said Heinrich Heine, and few are geniuses when the books' editor and his minions get to work. Mark Twain said that reviews are chloroform in print, and fortunately these days, negative criticisms seem to have little effect, as the internet and the voices of the readers take over.

To illustrate this, here are two quotes from later in my life, picked up while standing at the corner of the bar by the window at the Garrick, and listening to Kingsley Amis before he was helped to the coffee room for a late lunch. One: 'Yes, his book, once put down, was hard to pick up,' and, more encouragingly to any author, his much admired remark, 'Critics have spoiled my breakfast, but never my lunch.' Amen to that.

Such sentiments lead to a brief reflection on the dangers of modern computer technology, when an author friend decided to give a character in one of his novels a new name, replacing 'David' with the workaday 'Fred', in a nearly completed manuscript. He pressed the appropriate keys to make the automatic changes throughout the entire text. Only later, at proof stage, did he notice that the heroine travelled to Florence where she marvelled at the great statue of Michelangelo's Fred.

I usually brief myself as I get to know someone, but sometimes the details get lost. I was privileged to become friends with another Fred, the famous film director Fred Zinnemann, and we had frequent lunches together, usually in Langans, off Piccadilly, where he always ordered sausage and mash. He invited me, and my wife, to the Austrian Embassy when he received an honour from the ambassador of the country of his birth. When the discredited Kurt Waldheim became Austria's President, Zinnemann returned the honour and called on us again to mark the occasion.

Fred commissioned me to do a treatment for a film project he was interested in developing, about how the British, in his view, had betrayed the Cossacks by handing them over to the Soviets and certain death, after the Second World War. Having researched his professional life less well than I should have done, I asked him whether, since he had made such classics as *High Noon*, *The Nun's Story* and *The Day of the Jackal*, what he would still like to do? Would he ever think of doing a musical, for instance?

'I did one once, Michael,' he said with a gentle smile. 'It was called *Oklahoma*.'

Fred also told me the story about the director of *Death in Venice* driving through, say, Wolverhampton, on a nasty cold wet night. He passed a deserted-looking cinema that was showing his film. At the doorway, he saw the cinema manager, in a frayed dinner-jacket, standing miserably by the door, so he stopped the car, got out, and asked the man how *Death in Venice* was doing.

'As well as Death in Wolverhampton would do in Venice,' came the disgruntled reply.

Zinnemann was a genuinely modest man, with modesty a far from commonplace factor in public life. One other genuinely modest man stands out in my memory. With more hereditary titles than almost any other in British society – where titles can still matter – he was Earl of Arundel, Baron Beaumont, Baron Maltravers, Earl of Surrey and Baron Howard of Glossop, among many others, and he used to joke, in a most self-deprecating manner, that he had 'ten different seats in the House of Lords, but only one bottom to put on them'. He ruled on matters of State ceremony, telling The Queen and various archbishops of Canterbury, and not least prime ministers, what they could or could not do at great State occasions, yet he was also the most senior lay member of the Roman Catholic Church in Britain. Miles Fitzalan-Howard, the 17th Duke of Norfolk, was a truly modest man, wise and helpful to me on many occasions, and, above all, funny, though even some of his closest family did not realise, until they read it in his obituaries, that he had won the Military Cross for heroism in France during the Second World War.

Modesty again, and a call on that sparkling but morose-looking man Joseph Luns, the former Secretary-General of NATO, to prepare for a visit by The Queen to NATO Headquarters, before going on to the European Commission in Brussels. Of the Commission Chief, Roy Jenkins, all that one was left with was a general feeling that Mr Jenkins was so much grander than any of his visitors. But as for Mr Luns, who was the longest ever serving Secretary-General, he was a joy to be with. On the reconnaissance trip he met the small advance party in his grand office, wearing a tartan rug wrapped round his waist like a kilt 'to keep the draughts off', while on his feet he wore a pair of the most threadbare of carpet slippers. 'But I do have shoes,' he said. 'I promise I'll wear them for Her Majesty.'

After my Palace days, I worked for James Hanson and Gordon White for some years, and a dynamic experience that was. The two of them were a case of one and one equalling six when they were together, working hard and playing hard, with a lot of laughter between the tensions. Their fellow businessmen at the time put them at the top of their list of best entrepreneurs, with a company 'from over here, doing rather well over there' on the other side of the Atlantic. One learned a lot, listening to other top businessmen like Lord Hanson's friend Lord King, Chairman of British Airways, and the mega-rich Lord Rothschild, who despite his fortune, turned up to lunch one day with the insouciance that only vast wealth can bring, with huge Charlie Chaplin-sized holes in the soles of both shoes, which actually showed the socks beneath. Then there was Sir James Goldsmith, who, because he had been delayed by bad weather on one occasion in the first-class lounge at Heathrow, I sat chatting to at more length than I might otherwise have expected. One thing I remember from the conversation was his remark that 'The most dangerous man in any company is one who is totally dedicated, hard-working, late working, loyal and wrong.'

Hanson and White were invited to a private preview of *Wall Street*, since Michael Douglas's part, playing the corporate raider Gordon Gecko, was meant to be based on Gordon White's New York business style. As they left, they said to the worried producer, 'Michael Shea will tell you what we think of it.' As they never told me, I never knew.

I went to Claridge's with Lord Hanson for lunch one day, for a meeting about Melody Radio, the franchise which we had bid for and won. As we entered, an elegant lady of a certain age came up to James, and, kissing him warmly on both cheeks, said, somewhat to his surprise, 'Oh I am so glad to see you. I thought you died last week.'

It was a good opener to a very brief conversation. 'Who the hell was that and what was she talking about?' Lord Hanson asked later. I could answer the second question but not the first. From a brief aside I realised she had just read the obituary of the creator of the *Muppets*, Jim Henson, in the press.

Working at corporate, as opposed to Palace, communications was not just better paid, it was something of an eye-opener. Much was different, much was the same. The private sector was, at the time, held to be more dynamic, more with it, more alert and sparkly in communicating with the outside world. Sometimes it was, sometimes it was not. At about that time I started my extensive collection of corporate, commercial absurdities, the collapse of the reputations of companies from British Gas to Ratners, through the follies of poor public relations. These large-scale disasters have been well covered and documented, but, as always, it is the small things that make the impact on the public at large. Among them are a few examples of why we no longer need court jesters to make us laugh, particularly when the marketeers are trying to excel themselves in the social responsibility stakes.

Take Tesco peanuts, even today: turn the package around and you'll see the information in big bold letters: 'Warning: Contains Peanuts'.

On a hermetically sealed package containing one green pepper, the information reads, 'Product of more than one country'.

With a child's folding pram comes the instruction, 'Do not fold while child is seated in it'. Or, on Tesco's oranges, 'Ideal for eating'; on fly-killer, 'not tested on living creatures'; on Boots' sunglasses, 'Do not use in bright sunlight'; and on a pack of 'Genuine Smoky Back-bacon flavoured crisps' the encouragement, 'Suitable for vegetarians'.

But my favourite example of all concerns a Norwegian brand of bottled glacier water. On the outside the label reads 'This purest of pure water comes from a glacier that has been frozen for a million years.' At the bottom one reads 'Best before June 2003'. And these are the commercial world's duties of public information and safety writ large.

Circumstances of time and geography fundamentally changed an old university friend when I met him years later at the Yak and Yeti Hotel, in Katmandu. I was visiting Nepal to make arrangements for the forthcoming State Visit by The Queen. My friend had been awarded his PhD in Edinburgh with great distinction. He was a liberated man, who became a Cabinet Minister for Education in Nepal, until those selfsame liberal instincts led to his downfall. He told me once that he had trekked for seven days as a child to get to his first elementary school. In Britain, he campaigned for every human right under the sun. But when I dined at his house that night, the table was only set for two – or three for a while, for his ten-year-old son briefly joined us. His wife and daughter, however, smiling and welcoming, stood silently behind our chairs and served us throughout the meal. I remember that I began to say something, perhaps to argue, or offer his wife my chair, but I held my peace. It would have been out of place.

Sitting on the sidelines watching the pompous of all sorts and conditions is a great breeding-ground for side-splitting humour. Ridicule destroys more completely than the most reasoned attack. I sat beside that gentle man, Geoffrey Howe, when he travelled as British Foreign Secretary on a State Visit with The Queen to China. We were in first-class seats together, just behind the royal cabin on the VC10. I had been laughing at a book of political quotations I had just bought, and handed it to him when he asked what I found so funny. He quickly handed it back to me without opening it. 'Very droll,' he said. Only then did I note that the only quote on the front cover was Dennis Healey's famous one about Geoffrey, that an attack by him was like being 'savaged by a dead sheep'. It could have killed our conversation, but he shrugged my embarrassment aside and talked of his current problems with Europe and Mrs Thatcher's implacable hostility to further integration. He quoted

Napoleon to me, that the only way to unite Europe was to run an army back and forth across it every few years.

It was a period in British politics where the one-liner could destroy the man. Politicians, after all, try to ride the waves if they can, rather than make them, and avoid controversy. But some say so much that ridicule is inevitable. Thatcher versus Kinnock, 'the handbag versus the windbag'; Kenneth Baker, 'the future of the Tory party and it smirks', and so on are words that lead to the graveyards of political life.

But every age has had its repartee, rightly ensuring that politicians are never quite at ease with themselves; thus Oswald Mosley on Stanley Baldwin as 'the yawn personified', or Curzon on the same much maligned figure as being 'a man of the utmost insignificance'. Comedians of all ages destroy more than any opposition. I have delighted in meeting and working with several of them. John Wells, one of the founders of the Establishment Club in the Soho of the sixties, which was set up to undermine and ridicule the 'Establishment' I described earlier, later in life created a personality greater than Mrs Thatcher's husband could ever be in his play *Anyone for Dennis*. I worked on a television proposal with him and John Cleese, and I have never laughed so much. Trying to compete with their humour was pointless, with the latter silencing my own meagre effort at telling a funny story, with 'Michael, you've just given new meaning to the expression *Shea's longue*.'

And then there is Jeffrey Archer. He thought he was at the epicentre of the Establishment, but his judgement was flawed on that score as well. One thing he did have, however, was an amazing rabble-rousing fluency. At a Tory Party Conference – Blackpool or Brighton, it doesn't matter – Norman Lamont, as Chancellor of the Exchequer, made a long, lacklustre speech. He sat down to nil applause, and nil means nil. Then Jeffrey Archer bounced on to the platform, as only Jeffrey could, and the Conference went wild. As with Arthur Scargill, the mob listened to the loudest voice. Even before he had opened his mouth to raise funds, or to tell everyone in the hall what splendid people they all were, they cheered him to the rafters. Do those who were there remember baying to that illusion?

Perhaps this is as good a place as any to mention other party conferences I had attended as an impartial observer for the huge company that employed me. On the sidelines on these occasions, one could only note how the political mirrors both reflected reality and deceived. The sidelines were the only place to sit, to take in the inevitability of it all. Particularly over the last decade and a half, there have been few soaring speeches, and the applause for the party leaders has become more and more dutiful rather than enthusiastic. Take the 1995 Tory Conference, for example. There were fewer people, fewer parties of a social sort, fewer outstanding speeches and standing ovations, fewer outside observers, because it no longer mattered to industry and their lobbyists whether they attended, because nothing of any significance was going to happen.

Behind the window-dressing, the shops were bare, and the 'Vision Thing' was long gone, with the gaps between the parties more or less extinguished. Yes, the slogans were still all on display, examples of 'Forward with the People', 'One Nation' nonsense, all equally meaningless and banal. And the same with the Labour Party. Tony Blair is too busy these days. He is a victim of his own success and has to keep going; so, not unnaturally, he cannot waste time campaigning at conferences against those below him. At the time of writing he still looks the part and sounds the part, a wolf that is never going to be overcome no matter how many sheep there are around, though if I were to advise him, I would suggest that he paused more for dramatic effect, giving his audience time to think and go with his flow. His only recent memorable predecessor, Mrs Thatcher, was even more of a conviction politician than he is, but she did not employ Tim Bell and the Saatchis to bolster her convictions, only to perfect her presentation. As an observer, no longer having to handle the press corps or be polite to the editors who turned up for the leaders' speeches, I particularly relished the often funny and always destructive riot of cynicism, and the mockery, which they used in their whispered commentaries on such occasions. If you frogmarched squads of young people of today, who are accused of being uninterested in politics, to these conferences, and forced them to listen to a day or so of pitiless platitudes, you would inoculate them against the system for the rest of their lives.

Observing our present political condition from the sidelines, we can note, without too much surprise, that there are, consequently, more members of the Royal Society for the Protection of Birds than of all British political parties put together, and that, at time of writing, more people voted for a TV programme called 'Pop Idol' than voted at the last general election. In such circumstances, when Rory Bremner claims that the present clutch of ministers, in their off-the-peg designer suits, think of farming as vineyards and olive groves, everyone laughs because it is nearly true.

I have been unable to track down the origin of a remark which goes as follows: 'The progress of political evolution, from Gladstone and Disraeli, to today's political leaders, contains evidence enough to upset Darwin.' At a guess, a lot of people have made similar remarks. Contemporary political debate, particularly in the House of Commons, with all its studied theatricals, too often seems like bald men fighting over a toothless comb, since so little clear blue sea lies between the major participants. On most major issues, any clear water that does exist is stirred up until it is grey and muddy, so that no amount of 'management of illusion' has much effect on the electorate. This creates, rather, disillusion, giving rise to a situation where the media becomes the feared opponent of government, where tomorrow's headlines are far more critical to and of a government's reputation than anything mouthed by mere Opposition leaders. Editors become the king-makers, but they are also the clown-makers, and once the pack starts snapping around a politician's ankles and laughing at him at the same time, he or she is done for. Look how they felled Michael Portillo, Peter Mandelson and a dozen others like them.

It is impossible to mock the media or to be their enemy: they perform both functions so well themselves. The puppy dogs of war eat other puppy dogs, and most will eat themselves for a front-page headline. Sometimes a participant in the conflict, but usually sitting on the sidelines, I have seen the worst so often destroy the best.

That great former *Washington Post* correspondent in London, Johnny Apple, once said to me: 'I'm not in the same profession as 95 per cent of British journalists.' I recognised at once what he was talking about, the irresponsible mix of fact and opinion that is printed daily as the truth.

Mastery of the facts and knowledge of the subject being covered, except for some expert correspondents, is seldom more than half an inch deep with many journalists. As Jeremy Paxman has written, a foreign correspondent's in-depth research, for example, too often consists of 'reading the relevant back-issue of *Time* magazine on the place . . . and then getting hold of the number of the local Reuters bureau'. Again and again I found, when briefing journalists at the beginning of a foreign tour, I was being asked, not about The Queen and the details of the trip, but about the country concerned, its capital, its leaders, and, of course, its current controversies. One evening in the late seventies, I actually stopped a journalist filing a vivid, apparently first-hand description of the Duke of Edinburgh going lion hunting in India (no: there were no lions in India), and, on another occasion, prevented one tabloid journalist filing a story about a royal visit to a country that we were not actually visiting. The man was indignant rather than grateful when I put him right. 'Why the hell didn't you tell me we weren't in Iran?' he complained.

Some press were irrepressible. For some reason, now forgotten, during a visit to New Zealand, Harry Arnold of the *Sun* irritated the then Prime Minister, Mr Muldoon, who was widely known as Piggy Muldoon. At a press conference the PM angrily denounced British tabloid journalists as a bunch of 'ratbags'. 'What's a ratbag?' asked Arnold. 'You' replied the Prime Minister. Unabashed, Arnold's stories from New Zealand for the next few days were all bylined in print as being from 'Harry Ratbag Arnold'.

The royal family are remarkably unshockable. They have been everywhere, seen everything, but it still took me quite a time to assure my friend David Nicholas, the then editor-in-chief of ITN, a man branded the 'life-force' of independent television news for more than a quarter of a century, that no offence had been taken during a private visit by The Queen to watch *News at Ten* go out. We had decided on ITN rather than BBC, because while David knew she was coming, it remained his secret. Had we gone to the BBC, despite the best efforts of the great Cliff Morgan, at that time head of Royal Liaison, everyone would have known, and The Queen would have been met by the Chairman and Governors, the Director-General and a hundred others as well. By contrast, private visits to ITN – and I arranged ones for the Princess of Wales and for Princes Andrew and Edward as part of a familiarisation programme, never leaked until the visit was well under way.

That particular night, David Nicholas brought The Queen into the darkened control room just as the news was going on air. Those who have been there know that tensions can run high. There was the odd cock-up and the well-known news editor – I will spare her blushes – unaware of who had come in to stand quietly behind her, turned the air blue with her vocabulary. David tried to warn her, but she had the programme to get out, and her boss was ignored. She camouflaged her embarrassment later, particularly when The Queen remarked that, with husband and sons in the Navy, the words that had floated through the ether were hardly new to her.

To sum up, the media class are, by and large, more important than the political class. They have a love affair with fame and celebrity, but it does not last. The press needs its victims, and many careers, from film stars and footballers to cabinet ministers, are in the gift of the tabloids. They are particularly good at coming down from the hills and shooting the wounded. They can always find someone, a rent-a-rant MP or other hairy-chested tub-thumper, to give them a quote that will add petrol to any smouldering resentment, or to be furious about any issue. Mrs Thatcher was quoted as saying that fury was, at times, the only emotion she was allowed by the media. Ditto The Queen, a lady, as I have said elsewhere, never known for being furious about anything. But fury *is* a good, short, four-letter word, for those paragons of accuracy, the newspaper headline writers.

ELEVEN

A Spindoctor Writes

Never underestimate facts. They can flower into a truth.

Emerson

Mark Twain proclaimed that we all know for certain many facts that are simply not true. 'Facts, or what a man believes to be facts, are delightful. . . . Get your facts first,' he wrote, 'and then you can distort them as much as you please.' In similar vein, I remember Brian Walden, the political journalist, stating that little of what we think we know about the famous is true. The up-to-the-moment word is a 'factoid', an assumption or speculation reported and repeated so often that it is popularly considered to be correct. It is, for example, how the Moral Majority is created.

There is an old story of a Scottish king, who is sitting on his throne when he receives a battle-weary knight. The latter kneels before him and says, 'Sir, I have been raping and pillaging among your enemies in the south.'

'But I have no enemies in the south,' replies the king. To which the decisive response comes, 'By God, Sir, you have now!'

The media's energies are so often worthy of greater things than stirring up conflict, so why are facts not supported more widely and lies publicly dismissed as such? Sometimes they are; but why spoil a good story with the truth? When I was at Buckingham Palace, some tabloid journalists commonly used the expression TGTC, meaning 'too good to check', because if they did, the story would immediately be denied or disproved.

I recently came across a most useful Jewish word, *tummler*, meaning a decoy or a diversion, as used in the story of the young girl at boarding school who wrote to her parents to say that she had fallen in love with the gardener's boy, had been meeting him secretly behind the sports pavilion, was in love, was pregnant by him, and that they intended to run away together. As a postscript she added that none of the above was true, but that she had just failed her mock O-level maths and she wanted her parents to get that piece of news into proper perspective.

It is always a matter of perspective. There is always some drama going on in public life, with one person or other at centre stage. When that other girl sent her notorious e-mail suggesting that 11 September was a good day to bury bad news, she was merely reflecting what, off the record, every single professional press officer or PR manager who had a downside story about to break would also have thought privately. The difference was that they did not get caught. It is the way of the world, and is done all the time, not just by governments, but by any organisation in the public or the private sector, with difficult news to impart. Just as dictators, or directors of failing companies, find external enemies or threats to blame, even in our private lives we all look for worse news elsewhere under whose lee to shelter.

It was all a matter of perspective when Archbishop Robert Runcie, a most sociable and kindly man, who had won a Military Cross while serving in the Scots Guards during the Second World War for being an excellent marksman, which meant killing lots of Germans, addressed a lunch of national newspaper editors I also attended in a London hotel. The Primate, who was constantly being accused by his detractors of nailing his colours to the fence, told a mildly risqué joke. The then editor of the *Sun*, Kelvin Mackenzie, a man not widely known for the sexual restraint of his paper, stood up and left the room rather noisily, saying that he did not like archbishops telling dirty stories. And the editor of the *Sun* was right of course. George Bernard Shaw once said that if an archbishop were to state that God existed, it was all in a day's work. If he said that God did not exist, then something significant had been said. If that particular archbishop had had his personal spindoctor whispering under his mitre, he'd have spoken in other terms, and our perception of the man would have created a different reality.

In contrast with his public image, the perception I always had of Mackenzie's proprietor, Rupert Murdoch, was of a man of great charm, particularly when The Queen came to visit *The Times*. On that occasion, Murdoch was openly critical of one of his editors for pushing his own ego, and changing the layout of his newspaper too frequently. 'Readers want to know where the marmalade is when they start their morning,' was his percipient remark. When I persuaded him to talk further about that editor, he admitted that he was going to be a difficult man to get rid of.

'So how do you go about it?' I daringly asked.

'Praise, promote, fire,' he replied convincingly, meaning that once you had promoted a man beyond his abilities, it was easy. Which is precisely what he did some time later.

I have had the mixed challenges and pleasures of trying to spin a particular line with several past editors of *The Times*. I went to lunch with Harry Evans and his editorial team sometime in the early eighties for example, and I remember arriving full of complaints about the behaviour of the tabloids, and in particular their photographers, in their hounding of certain junior members of the Royal Family. We had a bit of an argument about whether such editors could deny responsibility for the behaviour of the more aggressive freelance paparazzi, when most of the latter were being paid a daily brown envelope retainer to offer those very newspapers a first exclusive on anything they shot. 'When is a staff photographer not a staff photographer?' I asked.

Harry Evans brushed it all aside, saying that it was not a matter for him; *The Times* was different. They seldom – he was talking about the early eighties – covered royal stories outside the Court page.

I had done my homework, or at least my assistant at the Palace
had. 'So, apart from the Court page,' I asked, 'how many royal
stories are you covering today?'

'Can't remember any,' Harry responded. 'Maybe one . . . two?'

I had my answer. 'Thirteen', I said. *The Times* staff were
dispatched to check. We settled on twelve. A story on Prince Rainier
and the House of Grimaldi, in comparison to the House of Windsor,
did not count.

It was always fascinating studying the DNA of the media. At
lunch one day, my benevolent perception of Rupert Murdoch
rapidly changed over his treatment of an editor who was not even
from his stable. I was a lunch guest of Sir John Junor, who was in
his final phase as editor of the *Sunday Express*. He was one of
several newspaper editors, along with David English of the *Daily
Mail* and Larry Lamb of the *Sun* (of all papers) to have been
knighted, on the recommendation of Mrs Thatcher, doubtless in
the belief that they were 'one of us'. It was an odd practice that
has largely gone out of fashion. Perhaps she, or her press
secretary, Bernard Ingham, failed to hear what these editors said
about her in private.

Normally it was L'Escargot at which John Junor and I dined, or a
little Italian place in the Strand, but this time we met at Le Tour
d'Argent, to the north of Oxford Street. He could be both sycophant
and bully in his dealings with the Palace, and, if it is true that men
over fifty have the faces they deserve, John, a decade older than that,
was purple-faced and flushed, from a long life of drink, infidelity
and frequently amusing prejudice. Those under him, and he had
learned this from one of his first bosses, Beaverbrook, either bowed
or broke. He told me the latter's famous remark about some sex
scandal – 'Don't these politicians realise that Old Masters are a
better investment than young mistresses?' He was hugely critical of
one of his fellow editors, a man also knighted by Mrs Thatcher,
who, he said, seemed so dishonestly flexible that he might have been
following Groucho Marx's remark, 'These are my principles, and if
you don't like them, I have others.' Junor certainly had principles of

a sort, but he shocked me once by saying that friendship in the newspaper world was always far more corrupting than money or power. He hated his journalists becoming too chummy with politicians or others they were writing about, which is a fine argument, but the way he used the word 'friendship', as if it were a sickness, troubled me.

That particular lunch-time, Rupert Murdoch was sitting at an adjacent table with another well-known newspaper magnate. He had waved distantly to me as he came in. As we finished our meal, Junor said, 'Let's go and chat to them.' I thought that might not be very clever and I suggested as much, but Junor confidently advanced on Murdoch's table.

Murdoch looked up and made the most calculatingly dismissive gesture, with a flip of his wrist and hand, I have ever seen, and turned his back on Junor. Purple-faced Junor went white and crumpled. I have never seen a man's bubble of self-esteem burst so quickly.

Other times, other glimpses of attempted media manipulation – me of them and them of me – emerge from a jumble of the past. Within weeks of arriving at the Palace, I was invited to a party given by the Hickey column of the *Daily Express*, and, after some hesitation, I went along, since it was just across Green Park at the Ritz. As I went in, I met the effervescent Willy Rushton of *Private Eye*, one of the great cartoonists and broadcasters of the age, and we stood in a corner of the room talking to each other. Then I noticed, out of the corner of my eye, that one of the hosts of the evening was beginning to steer quite an attractive if ageing woman in my direction, and I also noticed that a couple of paparazzi photographers were taking up position as if to photograph me. Willie Rushton whispered a quick word of warning in my ear. I was about to be set up. A photograph of The Queen's new Press Secretary, in intimate conversation with Mandy Rice Davies of Profumo scandal fame, in the next day's *Express* might not have gone down too well with my stuffier colleagues the following morning. I made my excuses and left, remembering as I walked along Piccadilly the story, told me I think by Bill Deedes, of his hurrying along that same street one evening on his way to theatre, in the days when ladies of the night awaited their customers in every doorway. One woman came out of the shadows towards him, and he brushed her aside with some sort of 'not tonight, dear,' remark.

It was only when he had gone some few paces further on, that he realised that the woman, no, the lady, had been his proprietor's wife. What to do? Go back, find her, say 'I'm sorry, but I thought you were . . .'?

One of the key attempts at imposing some sort of self-discipline on the media during my time at Buckingham Palace took place shortly before Christmas 1981. We decided to invite in all the editors of the national newspapers, plus the editors of the BBC and ITN, to appeal to them to leave the Princess of Wales and other members of the royal family alone. It was the first gathering of its kind in almost a quarter of a century. Press harassment had become the major issue between the Palace and the media, and something had to be done about it, since there were even worries about how the constant harrying might affect the Princess's pregnancy. The other constant issue was to do with the civil list and royal finances, but as we were becoming more open and transparent about our costs than most government departments, that was assuming less and less importance in the public debate.

Having been involved in radio in my life, and having served on the Independent Television Commission for several years, I have to declare an interest, but I had, in my time, very little complaint when it came to coverage by the electronic media. There are many criticisms to be made of radio and television, and the latter sometimes forgets, to quote the late Huw Wheldon, that it should have as its objective 'to make the good popular and the popular good', but the electronic media paled and pales into insignificance when compared to the newspapers. From this I again generally exempted the regional press, for they, being more closely answerable to their constituents or readers, always showed a much greater responsibility and degree of accuracy in their reporting. But for the tabloids, no holds were barred when it came to the privacy of members of the royal family. Nothing was taboo, and the press complaints body of the day, like its successor, was a busted flush, and any policy of self-regulation and self-restraint was in tatters. It always was a chimera. Who could have expected anything else, composed as that so-called restraining body was, in part, of some of the very editors who were the principal culprits, held loosely together by weak or lacklustre chairmen? Subsequent governments have failed miserably to do anything about that, any more than they have put an end to the nasty business of chequebook journalism. Has this been because of a mistaken adherence to a culture of fanatical toleration of certain extremes of behaviour, or is it fear of becoming victims of the press themselves? The facts answer that very clearly indeed.

Concerns over matters of personal privacy, not just for the royal family, but for anyone in the public eye, should be one of any regulatory body's most important functions, given that, in the words of one Lord Chief Justice, 'the freedom of the press should prevail'. But, as Baroness O'Neill said in her 2002 Reith Lectures, 'the press has acquired unaccountable power that others cannot match,' and went on, 'A free press can be an accountable press . . .' since '. . . accountability does not require, indeed it precludes, censorship.' But, she added, 'freedom of the press also does not require a licence to deceive'. From a brilliant lecture, which I heard her expound at length, let me add one final quote: 'The press are skilled at making material accessible, but erratic about making it assessable.'

My meeting with the editors took place on a snowy December day, in great civility, in the 1844 Room in the Palace, and only one editor failed to attend. Kelvin Mackenzie claimed that he had a meeting with his proprietor, Rupert Murdoch, but he told me, and several hundred others, in a speech in Edinburgh long afterwards, that later that same afternoon he got a call from Murdoch who was in fact in the States, and who had already heard that he had been used as an excuse, to tell Mackenzie that if he was going to refuse invites from the Palace in the future, to leave him out of it.

I found the meeting informative, if only because while their staff journalists hunted in the same packs all the time, I had to introduce the then editor of the *Daily Mail* to the editor of the *Daily Express*, as they had never met.

We had our meeting: it has been written about in several books, and, as the then editor of *The Times*, Harry Evans, took a note of what was being said in shorthand, I cannot dispute it. It reports me as having asked them to get their photographers to back off, since 'She [Diana] will be part of the history of this country longer than any of us,' and that 'it would be a tragedy if her worries about the media were to continue into mature life . . .'. That future happened as I predicted, but, for the moment, the editors promised to pull their photographers off, and it was then that I told them that The Queen would like to invite them for a drink in the Carnarvon Room after the meeting. It was on that occasion, when the editor of the *News of the World* unthinkingly suggested to The Queen that if Diana did not like being photographed when she went shopping for winegums in Tetbury, 'why didn't she send a footman?' The Queen replied to the effect that that was the most ill-considered and pompous remark she had ever heard. The subsequent ridicule did for that editor's future career in newspapers. Dog eats dog in that kindly profession.

And how long did the stand-off last? Not long. 'There is no more fissile substance than a conglomerate of editors', wrote Harry Evans, and who am I to disagree?

Spindoctors, those creatures of the night, seem always to have been in the news. Yet as recently as 1995, when I took the manuscript of my new thriller, *Spindoctor*, to my very experienced publisher, he asked me, puzzled, what the term meant. Some reviewers subsequently suggested that I had invented the expression. While normally happy to accept such acclaim, I confessed I did not invent it, I had merely imported it from the United States where it did not have the pejorative sense it has in Britain today. I first heard it used by Michael Deaver, Deputy Chief of Staff in Ronald Reagan's White House, a man who also introduced me to the word 'mediagenic', a term, thankfully, that so far has not been much exported to the United Kingdom. When I asked him to define spindoctoring, Deaver said that a good example was his getting President Reagan to go all the way to China 'to be mediagenically photographed on a Wall'.

Because Reagan was known to be unconcerned with detail, Deaver, until his downfall, was widely known as a spindoctor with a crucial role. *Time* magazine, in August 1984, said that 'for all his personal influence, Deaver chooses to behave more like a steward of the presidential image than a shaper of public policy. He is the Master of the Household, the Lord Chamberlain of the White House'. I believe that I suggested those transatlanticised royal titles to *Time*, because I had seen at first hand how he operated, largely through Nancy Reagan, knowing how she would tend to react in any given situation. Deaver was in the Equerry's Room at Buckingham Palace in January 1986 when we heard that the NASA spaceship *Challenger* had exploded, killing everyone on board. Within minutes, he was on to the White House, not to speak to the President, nor any of the senior staff, but to Mrs Reagan, to tell her how the public pronouncements of grief should be drafted and handled.

While the word itself has had a short history, there is nothing particularly new in political spindoctoring. Even the term has its partial British antecedents, for I recently came across a reference to someone on Lloyd George's staff at 10 Downing Street, in 1917, talking about 'doctoring the news'. Since then there have been many prime ministerial press secretaries, like Joe Haines and Trevor Lloyd Hughes, who worked for Harold Wilson, and Tim Bell, Gordon Reece, Ronnie Miller and Bernard Ingham, who worked with Mrs Thatcher. Each one of them, while disclaiming that they were spindoctors, did exactly the same job. Why? Because governments of all complexions have always spent an inordinate amount of time on presentation, in order to ensure that the best possible construction is put on their actions and achievements. Nothing has or will change in that respect. And behind the spindoctors were the other hands that guided. In Mrs Thatcher's case, names like Kenneth Stowe, Clive Whitmore, Robin Butler, Nigel Wicks and Charles Powell were the senior civil servants, there to steer the hand that led the land. There were others too, turncoats from the left, like Paul Johnson who had been editor of the *New Statesman*, and the former communist, Alfred Sherman, not to mention the ubiquitous former Labour MP Woodrow Wyatt, a man rarely starved of an opinion or a prejudice. There were none like these converts for embracing Thatcherism at its purest, though it is interesting, to those of my age group, that while we probably come across one or two admitted ex-communists, never do we meet ex-fascists.

Shortly after they came to office, New Labour in their turn were reported to be set on using something called the 'Knowledge Network Project', whose objective was 'to explain the government's message directly to the public without going through the distorting prism of media reporting'. That was a quote worth very careful thought, since it is not so much a prism, but binoculars and a microscope that are needed for reporting and interpreting the political facts of life. Dressing words and actions properly, correcting unfortunate details, like a jacket buttoned up in the wrong holes – it is the little things that capture the next morning's headlines. Plutarch in his wisdom wrote, 'very often an action of small note, a short saying or a jest, shall distinguish a person's real character more than the greatest sieges or the most important battles', with Napoleon adding that 'the outcome of the greatest events is always determined by a trifle'. As a last resort, my advice to those I worked for has always been that a closed mouth gathers no feet, and if you are not sure what to say, and if you do not want to flirt with the truth, then silence can be a splendid option to take.

'We know no spectacle so ridiculous as the British public in one of its periodical fits of morality,' wrote Macaulay in the *Edinburgh Review* of June 1831, while reviewing a biography of Lord Byron. It could have been written in this, or any contemporary June. Add to that Disraeli's remark that what was called 'public opinion' is generally 'public sentiment', and you have in a nutshell today's fluctuations in the concerns of the nation. (The best story about Disraeli and communications concerns him on his deathbed, being asked if Queen Victoria, who was devoted to him, might come to pay him a last visit. 'Please, no,' came the reply. 'She will just give me a message for Albert.')

Presentation rules public life, and so there will be no move away from present practices while the media acts as the most immediate and effective opposition to those in power, by their manipulating of mass opinion on a daily basis. This explains why the Establishment's media teams grow ever stronger, as they are forced to grab control of at least some of the day's headlines.

Today's newspapers work in an environment where their readers have largely got the news from television or radio long before they bend down to pick up the paper from the front door mat. So, to hook them, editors have increasingly to tell the governors how to govern, and to censor their strategies as they see fit. Believing themselves superior to the politicians they patronise, and perhaps many are, they coil and interlace their own opinions round a story like a snake round its prey. After my experiences in Ghana and Romania, I can only be a great believer in a free press, and there is little point in the government of the day fulminating against such practices. They exist and have to be handled, for no one is going to put the clock back to the days where 'no comment' was the rule, and when the cold facts about any new government initiative were all that was issued from the other side of the media–government divide. Transparency is meant to rule and ministers and their little helpers, living in a world of false smiles, are forced to pander to the media and their demands to an inordinate degree. But if a sharp practitioner of the art of spinning becomes suspect and distrusted, that becomes an issue in itself and has to be dealt with. Perhaps people were cleverer in the old days.

What recent incumbent of Downing Street, with the possible exception of Edward Heath, was not thinking hard about how to affect the next morning's headlines by their public utterances when taking a key political decision? One of the most significant things that the former Chancellor, Norman Lamont, claimed when he resigned was that policy formulation at Number 10 always took second place to trying to manipulate the next morning's headlines.

Once of course it was different, and key political figures appeared to rise above such activity. Lord Kitchener, of whom Margot Asquith remarked 'He made a great poster', had a famously blunt approach in dealing with the press during the First World War. When bearded by them, his riposte was, 'Get out of my tent, you scum!'. Later, when Stanley Baldwin came under a sustained attack from the press, particularly those sections of it owned by the powerful newspaper barons of the day, his cousin, Rudyard Kipling, presented him with the famous quote, 'What these people want is power without responsibility – the prerogative of the harlot down the ages', and that helped his battle, at least for a while. Clement Attlee, in his turn, when asked if he was bothered about the newspapers and their criticisms of his policies, responded, 'Never read 'em', except, that was, for doing his daily crosswords. (Incidentally, press secretaries, and spokesmen for organisations inside and outside government, are in a position which is the complete reverse of newspapers: they have huge responsibilities to get things out on the right terms, but seldom have any power to achieve it.)

One of Macmillan's press aides, who had earlier worked for Anthony Eden, took me aside once when I was feeling particularly beleaguered by the press pack. He told me how Eden, whom Malcolm Muggeridge had dismissively called a 'public relations officer', had absolutely no time for journalists. He believed that paying any attention to what the press said warped the judgements he was called upon to make. My mentor told me how, at the height of the Suez crisis, Eden, who had declared 'we are not at war with Egypt; we are in armed conflict', had arrived back from a secret meeting in Paris, accompanied by his Foreign Secretary, Selwyn Lloyd. The two men flew into Biggin Hill aerodrome, to be met by a man from *The Times*, who had been tipped off about their arrival.

The man from *The Times* approached the Prime Minister, notepad in hand. The Prime Minister nodded distantly. The man from *The Times* asked the Prime Minister if he had anything to say to the newspapers. The Prime Minister turned to his Foreign Secretary. 'Selwyn, do we have anything to say to the newspapers?' he asked.

Selwyn Lloyd paused, then shook his head, 'No, Prime Minister. I don't think we have anything to say.'

'We have nothing to say to the press,' said Eden, turning back to the man from *The Times*.

'Thank you, Prime Minister,' the man from *The Times* responded politely. And that was that.

As I said at the beginning, Shakespeare had Malvolio divide leaders into those who were born great, those who acquired greatness, and those who had greatness thrust upon them. Today's climate adds a fourth category – those who appear great only as a result of the help of their spindoctors, public relations advisers, press secretaries and colour-me-beautiful gurus. When I quoted Lord Mancroft as saying that we are born equal but some of us manage to get over it, what he, too, could have added was, 'particularly if we're assisted by our personal spindoctor'.

A spindoctor builds up his or her client's ring of confidence, to make sure that they stand out in the crowd, and that what they say is listened to. I was a spindoctor if that means putting out my news, in my terms, at a timing of my choice. What press secretary or PR pundit does not do so, whether speaking for a government, a political party, a big multinational company or any other organi-sation in any Western democracy? We live in media-dominated societies where, on a daily basis, instant reputations are made or broken in the pages of the newspapers and on the television screens. Those whom editors would destroy, they first create as gods. Newspapers, particularly the tabloids, select certain mediagenic public figures, whether they be princes, prime ministers, pop stars or footballers. They build them up and have us worship them; then, when they get bored, or think their subjects are getting too big for their boots, or that they no longer pull the punters, they slaughter them before our eyes. It is the media that does most of the spinning of the cult of personalities in modern societies. As the journalist David Aaronovitch has written, political journalism is created by an incestuous clique who know all the same people and eat in the same places, which inevitably leads to a herd mentality that warps debate. They filter what they want to filter, whether it be news, culture, or gossip. In consequence, any leader of a commercial organisation or political party worthy of their salt is forced to get their backroom staff to manage the news that they put out, in an attempt to capture the right sort of attention. The media attack comes in a variety of guises. There is, for example, a type of hard but attractive woman journalist, who is, I believe, specially selected by her editor to go out and murder the people she is sent to interview. I have met three or four of the type in my life, and have suffered the consequences on more than one occasion. They smile, soften you up with praise, drink your tea or your alcohol, perhaps flirt a little, or test whether you would like to flirt with them, then they go away and write up their poison. Interviewees never learn, except sometimes. One American female of that genre – and why do women always make the best assassins? – was, on the other hand, so unprofessional as not to realise, when we had agreed that I was talking off the record, that a tape recorder, hidden in her bag, would bleep when the tape came to an end. I stopped talking immediately, asked for the tape, and when she refused to hand it over, I showed her the door and immediately rang her editor in New York. I'm glad to say she got the sack, not for using a tape recorder, but for not declaring it. Or was it because she was found out?

In circumstances where editors and their journalists throne and de-throne at will, organisations of all kinds are forced to hit back. They increasingly realise that the timing of an announcement is crucial, and that who says what, and how well they say it, is key. It is not necessary for their spindoctors to be economical with the truth, but they insist that they polish their version until it gleams. A benevolent view of a spindoctor's function is that an essential part of the process of government is to put across a clear and concise message. The downside of their calling comes with the stench of negative spin, blatant propaganda and all the muck that goes with it. Spinners know that denials don't work. You have got to get in first with the news, for if you have to go on the box or issue a press release denying that the minister was in a whore house, but was visiting his sick aunt instead, you know you're lost.

The fact is, denials don't work. Very early on in my time at the Palace, long before Lady Diana Spencer came on the scene, I was rung up late one night to be told that the first edition of the next morning's *Daily Express* was running as its front-page lead a story that Prince Charles was about to announce his engagement to Princess Marie Astrid of Luxembourg. New to the job, I incurred a fair amount of displeasure by waking up someone very senior to ask if there was any truth in the story. A few blown fuses later I issued a denial, via the Press Association, on the lines that not only was Prince Charles not going to get engaged to the Princess, but that it was far from certain whether he had even met her. All the *Express* did was to put a question mark at the end of the front-page headline, 'Charles to Marry Marie Astrid?' and to begin the story with the words, 'Despite Buckingham Palace denials, rumours continue to abound that Prince Charles is about to announce his engagement . . .'. And so on. Why spoil a good story with the facts?

In the goldfish bowl of political life, facts don't speak for themselves. They need to be interpreted. Everyone knows Marshall McLuhan's 'the medium is the message', but few know that he went on to add that, 'politics is being replaced by imagery. The politician abdicates in favour of his image, for it is more powerful than he could ever be.' That needed saying as well. Small men and women in the public eye need their media handlers if they are to survive and grow. Style triumphs over substance. Perception is the only reality.

The question is, what and who to believe? Why not, as you read this, scribble down a list of names of all those in public life whom you do instinctively believe? As a national serviceman, I used to listen to the British Forces Broadcasting Service, and from that I got hooked on its mentor, the BBC's World Service, a splendid organisation that has done so much good in keeping the world impartially informed over the past decades. Whether struggling to pick it up in West Africa on an inadequately tuned wireless and a poor aerial, or in Bucharest, when sometimes it was deliberately jammed, it became a challenge wherever I was posted and the theme tune of 'Lillibolero' haunts me to this day. More importantly, Mikhail Gorbachev is on record as saying that he only gave credence to the fact that a plot was being hatched against him in the Kremlin, while he was sunning himself at his Black Sea dacha, because he heard it reported on the BBC World Service's Russian programme. King Abdullah of Jordan, who was flying to the States at the time, did not believe that the events of 11 September were happening until his pilot insisted he listen to the BBC reports. Do we give our full trust to the Pope, The Queen, Mr Blair, Mr Duncan Smith, President Bush, Mr Mandela, Kate Adie, Trevor McDonald or Martin Bell? Do we implicitly accept as credible some anchormen and women on the news programmes more than others? This is not an easy question to answer. For years, millions believed in Stalin or Hitler, while the British believed in Churchill, the Free French in de Gaulle, and many Americans in Roosevelt. Political leaders and their spindoctors can fool some of the people some of the time. It is the job of the media to ensure that they don't fool all of the people all of the time.

I instigated and wrote a weekly column in a London evening paper for a while, under the title 'A Spindoctor Writes . . .'. My technique was to look at certain news events of the previous week and see how they could have been better handled from a media point of view. So often I saw a good case being badly presented, and there is nothing the media likes more than a botched PR job. At that time, there was a craze for dethroning the so-called fat-cat captains and kings of British industry. We had inarticulate bosses of water companies and British Gas being hounded out of office, not because they were doing a bad job, but because they put their public relations case so crassly. I found easy journalistic examples, as waves of politicians slipped on the banana skins of life, usually to do with dalliances outside marriage, which led to embarrassingly bad PR attempts to salvage their careers as they were briefly 'stood-by' by loyal wives and families.

People still ask whether, in my days at Buckingham Palace and elsewhere in the public and private sector, my way of operating was different from that of Mr Mandelson, Mr Campbell and their ilk in today's political circus. In one crucial respect it was different. In my day, political spokesmen, and poor press secretaries at Buckingham Palace, could make their carefully drafted utterances, but had no feeling of certainty that they would necessarily be backed up by those around them. I could not for a moment imagine, for instance, that the Princess of Wales was privately briefing one or two chosen members of the press corps about her view of the world, and later I was totally convinced that Andrew Morton did not have the true story he claimed to have. How wrong I was. Even those close to the action can be led astray. Nowadays, politicians are required to remain firmly 'online'. They ring up the centre of the cobweb to ask their own particular spider whether they are allowed to speak to the media on some issue. Some ministers are given their licence, and some are not. In the old days we used to joke that every time Gerald Kaufman appeared on television, another 100,000 people would change to vote Tory. That sort of thing happens no more. The weak are a long time in politics. Modern media handlers know this too well, and will keep their principals away from the microphones and the camera lenses unless they can play hardball. In today's world, Alastair Campbell makes Sir Bernard Ingham look soft.

On the subject of Bernard, he and I sparred a bit in the press in the autumn of 1995 about whether he had ever been a spindoctor, and more importantly, whether the next election would be won or lost by that breed handling their particular party of puppets. I suggested it would. He was a man I much admired when he was at Number 10, and equally when he made a caricature of himself when reviewing the newspapers on television. He sprang into print to say that I was wrong and that it was policies that would win, and that spindoctors, without them, were like weavers without weft.

I argued back. It would be the strategists, and their marketing and the presentation of their public image, which would win the day, no matter how good the manifestos on either side of the political chasm. The candidates could define these policies with the greatest attention to detail, but, sadly, such political facts would make little difference, unless they were carefully sanded and polished and put in the right place in the shop window. I believe I was right. Behind Tony Blair, Peter Mandelson proved my point.

There is yet another difference. Today's spindoctors are cleverer at looking for suitable news pegs with media appeal, largely because so many of them have served in that world. All editors have news holes to fill in any given day. A major disaster or the death of an important person will wipe most other news stories off the front pages. You cannot blame the editors: their main problem is which story to lead on. A little game the royal press pack used to play in days gone by was as follows: imagine, as a hack photographer or scribbler, you are in the middle of a huge room with two doors. They both open simultaneously. Standing at one end is a top-class source announcing a surprise royal engagement. At the other, similarly genuine, is someone offering an exclusive interview with a live Lord Lucan. Which way do you run?

When I left the Palace, the *Sun* devoted a whole editorial to me. Under the heading 'Bye, bye, Mike', it referred to me as the anti-Press Secretary, and said 'good riddance', or words to that effect. I have the item framed in my smallest room, together with the lead article on exactly the same page of that newspaper, under the banner headline 'The Wizard at the Palace', which told its readers what an outstanding star I had been and what wonderful changes I had made. 'Evidence on file' as they say, but such is the press. Face both ways, and don't give a damn; and remember that rising stars always become shooting stars in the end.

When one is making a speech two words waken up even the sleepiest of audiences: they are, 'In conclusion'! And so, in conclusion, was I ever economical with the truth? Perhaps, yes. Did I dissimulate, did I ever lie? No, never; well, almost never.

In conclusion, during a State Visit to Oman, The Queen and her entourage flew one day from Muscat, the capital, up to Firq, a remote mountain village. Disembarking from the Andover of The Queen's flight, and against the background of bleak, vegetation-free mountains and an ancient mud fort she was greeted by the Wali, or Vizier, of Firq himself. He was a splendidly turbaned, elderly man with an Abraham Lincoln beard, wearing a rich robe that billowed open to reveal a leather bandolier, strung with polished brass .303 bullets, from which also hung an elaborate silver dagger. Around him stood a sea of similarly dressed elders, while, in the background, there were veiled women, in bejewelled robes, all surrounded by beautiful barefoot children, watching and clapping their greetings. Then, despite the best laid plans of her security staff, The Queen herself was swept away by the dusty crowd of enthusiastic tribesmen, many of them firing off their ancient muskets into the air in friendly greeting.

The Duke of Edinburgh, naturally, does not like losing sight of The Queen in such circumstances, and, not best pleased, he climbed up on to the freshly dusted bonnet of a Land-Rover to see if he could spot her amid the throng.

Cut to that evening and my usual late-night press briefing of the eighty-strong travelling press corps about the events of the day. In response to a question from an excited tabloid journalist, did I hear myself say 'No, no. What the Duke actually said was, "Where IN FIRQ is The Queen?"'

Index